Headin' to the Cabin

Day Hiking Trails of Northwest Wisconsin

By Rob Bignell

Atiswinic Press · Ojai, Calif.

HEADIN' TO THE CABIN:
DAY HIKING TRAILS OF NORTHWEST WISCONSIN

Atiswinic Press
Ojai, Calif. 93023
hikeswithtykes.com/headintothecabin_home.html

ISBN 978-0-9858739-6-7
Library of Congress Control Number: 2013906439

Cover design by Rob Bignell

Manufactured in the United States of America
First printing April 2013

For Kieran

Table of Contents

Introduction

Ah, "headin' to the cabin" – those few words alone are enough to conjure images of a relaxing weekend by the lake, of a pleasant stroll through the woods or along a beach, of a place where one's cell phone hopefully doesn't work.

Whether you own a cottage that you visit on weekends or rent one for a week-long vacation, "headin' to the cabin" is more than a time-honored tradition among Twin Cities residents and Wisconsinites. Simply put, it's part of who we are.

After all, who can resist the sight of a white-tailed deer that freezes for a moment before us then darts into the brush just as we turn a corner? Or the sound of loons in the morning as the sun rises? The fragrant scent of wildflowers blossoming upon a secluded meadow you stumble upon? The taste of pan-fried fish caught just that morning in the lake? The feel of the warm night air as the stars shine in all their splendor above us?

A great way to experience all that "up north" has to offer is through day hiking. These are walks into the countryside that take only a couple of hours, giving you plenty of time to enjoy other activities during your weekend yet leave you invigorated.

Why day hike?

There are plenty of good reasons to go day hiking while at your cabin.

Chief among them is spending quality time with your family. The trail marks a place where you can grow closer, where unhindered by the distractions of mobile phone texts, emails, and the next television program, family members can talk with one another, where you can revel together in discovery. Hiking with your children can lead to a family tradition, experiences that later in life both parent and full-grown child will reminisce fondly about.

As humans, we need the natural world because we are incomplete without it. A walk alongside a lake or through a quiet forest allows us to get away from the pressures and hectic pace of modern life. Nature helps us relax and relieve stress. The sights of the natural world can raise our spirits and inspire us.

Hiking is a low-impact exercise that's energizing. It helps strengthen muscles, the heart and lungs, builds stamina and endurance. Exercise certainly is necessary, especially at a time of high obesity in the United States – but why limit yourself to walking alone on a treadmill inside a building when you could be with your family breathing in fresh balsam-scented air or feeling the breeze off Lake Superior run through your hair?

Rambling and exploring in nature can enrich our lives. We can delight in in the sight of soaring eagles and water gently flowing over rounded stones, sights we don't otherwise see in our lives. If with children, the experience is magnified. Kids notice things in nature that we adults have long taken for granted. A child can reawaken our wonderment of and appreciation for the natural world.

The trail is where children learn to enjoy, respect and love nature. Hearing the varied sounds of birds and feeling the splash of a waterfall against one's cheek builds the compassion that raises our children to become stewards of the natural world.

Indeed, kids exposed to the outdoors at an early age usually will love the outdoors through their lives. Hiking can be a fun, healthy, safe, social activity that they enjoy during their trying teen years. As they enter adulthood, their love of the trail can lead to mastering other outdoor activities, such as rock climbing, trail running, mountaineering, caving, canoeing, fishing, kayaking, skiing, snowshoeing, ice climbing and more.

Cabin-specific trails

While there are a lot of books about hiking trails, none of them are particularly helpful to cabin-goers. Many of the titles focus on long overnight backpacking excursions (But you purchased or rented a cabin to sleep in!) while other volumes merely list popular paths at state parks that often are more than a couple of hours drive away, meaning you'll spend more time on the road driving to and from the trail than actually hiking it.

No more.

The "Headin' to the Cabin" series focuses on trails that are close to the communities where cabin-goers frequently stay, whether it's because they own or rent. The trails also are short enough that you can spend a couple of hours on them, so you can enjoy a leisurely day and have plenty of time to do other stuff – or even sleep in the day you plan to hike!

This specific book in the series lists trails in northwestern Wisconsin, specifically the counties of Ashland, Barron, Bayfield, Burnett, Douglas, Polk, St. Croix, Sawyer and Washburn. Twin Citians as well as residents of southern Wisconsin and northern Illinois on vacation most commonly frequent northwestern Wisconsin cabins.

For each featured trail in this book, you'll find the following information:
- Best time to go
- Driving directions to the trail
- Any entry fees there may be
- Where to park and find the trailhead
- Course the trail takes
- Scenic points to look for on the trail
- Animals and flora you might spot
- Interesting tidbits about the area's geology and history

■ Any potential dangers to watch for

■ Trailside amenities, such as water fountains and bathrooms

In addition, for each community, you'll find a list of other excellent nearby trails that you might consider hiking.

Where are the maps?

One thing you won't find in this guidebook is maps. To properly prepare for any hike, you should examine maps before hitting the trail and bring them with you (see the Special Section for more). No guidebook can reproduce a map as well as the satellite pictures or topographical maps that you can find online for free. The companion website (*http://hikeswithtykes.com/headintothecabin_trailmaps.html*) to this book offers a variety of printable maps for each listed trail.

Since cabin-goers frequently are families, many of this book's trails are listed with kids in mind. Of course, children have clothing, gear and first-aid needs that differ from adults, so being aware of these matters is important for any enjoyable hike. To learn more about hiking with children, check out this author's "Hikes with Tykes" books or blog (*hikeswithtykes.com/home.html*). There you'll find all kinds of tips and fun games and activities that kids (and even adults!) will love.

All too often our cabin communities, whether we own or rent, are a little too much like the very urban areas we just left. While not quite as crowded and certainly more scenic, there's a whole world surrounding your cabin to explore. Go on – get out and see what awaits.

We'll see you on the trail!

Special Section: Hiking Northwest Wisconsin

You'll get more out of a day hike if you research it and plan ahead. It's not enough to just pull over to the side of the road and hit a trail that you've never been on and have no idea where it goes. In fact, doing so invites disaster.

Instead, you should preselect a trail (This book's trail descriptions can help you do that). You'll also want to ensure that you have the proper clothing, equipment, navigational tools, first-aid kit, food and water. Knowing the rules of the trail and potential dangers along the way also are helpful. In this special section, we'll look at each of these topics to ensure you're fully prepared.

Selecting a trail

For your first few hikes, stick to short, well-known trails where you're likely to encounter others. Once you get a feel for hiking, your abilities, and your interests, expand to longer and more remote trails.

Always check to see what the weather will be like on the trail you plan to hike. While an adult might be able to withstand wind and a sprinkle here or there, if you bring children, for them it can be pure misery. Dry, pleasantly warm days with limited wind always are best when hiking with children.

Don't choose a trail that is any longer than the least fit person in your group can hike. Adults in good shape can go 8-12 miles a day; for kids, it's much less. There's no magical number.

When planning the hike, try to find a trail with a mid-point payoff – that is something you and definitely any children will find exciting about half-way through the hike. This will help keep up everyone's energy and enthusiasm up during the journey.

If you have children in your hiking party, consider a couple of additional points when selecting a trail.

Until children enter their late teens, they need to stick to trails rather than going off-trail hiking, which is known as bushwhacking. Children too easily can get lost when off trail. They also can easily get scratched and cut up or stumble across poisonous plants and dangerous animals.

Generally, kids will prefer a circular route to one that requires hiking back the way you came. The return trip often feels anti-climatic, but you can overcome that by mentioning features that all of you might want to take a closer look at.

Once you select a trail, it's time to plan for your

day hike. Doing so will save you a lot of grief – and potentially prevent an emergency – later on. You are, after all, entering the wilds, a place where help may not be readily available.

When planning your hike, follow these steps:

- Print a road map showing how to reach the parking lot near the trailhead. Outline the route with a transparent yellow highlighter and write out the directions.
- Print a satellite photo of the parking area and the trailhead. Mark the trailhead on the photo.
- Print a topo map of the trail. Outline the trail with the yellow highlighter. Note interesting features you want to see along the trail and the destination.
- If carrying GPS, program this information into your device.
- Make a timeline for your trip, listing: when you will leave home; when you will arrive at the trailhead; your turn-back time; when you will return for the cabin in your vehicle; when you will arrive at your cabin.
- Estimate how much water and food you will need to bring based on the amount of time you plan to spend on the trail and in your vehicle. You'll need at least 2 pints of water per person for every hour on the trail.
- Fill out two copies of a hiker's safety form. Leave one in your vehicle.

■ Share all of this information with a responsible person remaining in civilization, leaving a hiker's safety form with them. If they do not hear from you within an hour of when you plan to leave the trail in your vehicle, they should contact authorities to report you as possibly lost.

Clothing

Footwear

If your feet hurt, the hike is over, so getting the right footwear is worth the time. Making sure the footwear fits before hitting the trail also is worth it. With children, if you've gone a few weeks without hiking, that's plenty of time for feet to grow, and they may have just outgrown their hiking boots. Check out everyone's footwear a few days before heading out on the hike. If it doesn't fit, replace it.

For flat, smooth, dry trails, sneakers and cross-trainers are fine; but if you really want to head onto less traveled roads or tackle areas that aren't typically dry, you'll need hiking boots. Once you start doing any rocky or steep trails – and remember that a trail you consider moderately steep needs to be only half that angle for a child to consider it extremely steep – you'll want hiking boots, which offer rugged tread perfect for handling rough trails.

Socks

Socks serve two purposes: to wick sweat away

from skin and to provide cushioning. Cotton socks aren't very good for hiking, except in extremely dry environments, because they retain moisture that can result in blisters. Wool socks or liner socks work best. You'll want to look for three-season socks, also known as trekking socks. While a little thicker than summer socks, their extra cushioning generally prevents blisters. Also, make sure kids don't put on holey socks; that's just inviting blisters.

Layering

On all but the hot, dry days, when hiking you should wear multiple layers of clothing that provide various levels of protection against sweat, heat loss, wind and potentially rain. Layering works because the type of clothing you select for each stratum serves a different function, such as wicking moisture or shielding against wind. In addition, trapped air between each layer of clothing is warmed by your body heat. Layers also can be added or taken off as needed.

Generally, you need three layers. Closest to your skin is the wicking layer, which pulls perspiration away from the body and into the next layer, where it evaporates. Exertion from walking means you will sweat and generate heat, even if the weather is cold. The second layer is an insulation layer, which helps keep you warm. The last layer is a water-resistant shell that protects you from rain, wind, snow and sleet.

As the seasons and weather change, so does the type of clothing you select for each layer. The first layer ought to be a loose-fitting T-shirt in summer, but in winter and on other cold days you might opt for a long-sleeved moisture-wicking synthetic material, like polypropylene. During winter, the next layer probably also should cover the neck, which often is exposed to the elements. A turtleneck works fine, but preferably not one made of cotton. The third layer in winter, depending on the temperature, could be a wool sweater, a half-zippered long sleeved fleece jacket, or a fleece vest.

You might even add a fourth layer of a hooded parka with pockets, made of material that can block wind and resist water. Gloves or mittens as well as a hat also are necessary on cold days.

Headgear

Half of all body heat is lost through the head, hence the hiker's adage, "If your hands are cold, wear a hat." In cool, wet weather, wearing a hat is at least good for avoiding hypothermia, a potentially deadly condition in which heat loss occurs faster than the body can generate it. Children are more susceptible to hypothermia than adults.

Especially during summer, a hat with a wide brim is useful in keeping the sun out of eyes. It's also nice should rain start to fall.

For young children, get a hat with a chin strap.

They like to play with their hats, which will fly off in a wind gust if not "fastened" some way to the child.

Sunglasses

Sunglasses are an absolute must if walking through open areas exposed to the sun, and in winter when you can suffer from snow blindness. Look for 100% UV-protective shades, which provide the best screen.

Equipment

A couple of principles should guide your purchases. First, the longer and more complex the hike, the more equipment you'll need. Secondly, your general goal is to go light. Since you're on a day hike, the amount of gear you'll need is a fraction of what backpackers shown in magazines and catalogues usually carry. Indeed, the inclination of most day hikers is to not carry enough equipment. For the lightness issue, most gear today is made with titanium and siliconized nylon, ensuring it is study and fairly light. While the list of what you need may look long, it won't weigh much.

Backpacks

Sometimes called daypacks (for day hikes or for kids), backpacks are essential to carry all of the essentials you need – snacks, first-aid kit, extra clothing.

For day hike purposes, you'll want to get yourself an internal frame, in which the frame giving the backpack its shape is inside the pack's fabric so it's not exposed to nature. Such frames usually are lightweight and comfortable. External frames have the frame outside the pack, so they are exposed to the elements. They are excellent for long hikes into the backcountry when you must carry heavy loads.

As kids get older, and especially after they've been hiking for a couple of years, they'll soon want a "real" backpack. Unfortunately, most backpacks for kids are overbuilt and too heavy. Even light ones that safely can hold up to 50 pounds are inane for most children.

When buying a daypack for your child, look for sternum straps, which help keep the strap on the shoulders. This is vital for prepubescent children as they do not have the broad shoulders that come with adolescence, meaning packs likely will slip off and onto their arms, making them uncomfortable and difficult to carry. Don't buy a backpack that a child will "grow into." Backpacks that don't fit well simply will lead to sore shoulder and back muscles and could result in poor posture.

Also, consider purchasing a daypack with a hydration system for kids. This will help ensure they drink a lot of water. More on this later when we get to canteens.

Before hitting the trail, always check your children's backpacks to make sure that they have not overloaded them. Kids think they need more than they really do. They also tend to overestimate their own ability to carry stuff. Sibling rivalries often lead to children to packing more than they should in their rucksacks, too. Don't let them overpack "to teach them a lesson," though, as it can damage bones and turn the hike into a bad experience.

A good rule of thumb is no more than 25 percent capacity. Most upper elementary school kids can carry only about 10 pounds for any short distance. Subtract the weight of the backpack, and that means only 4-5 pounds in the backpack. Overweight children will need to carry a little less than this or they'll quickly be out of breath.

Child carriers

If your child is an infant or toddler, you'll have to carry him. Until infants can hold their heads up, which usually doesn't happen until about four to six months of age, a front pack (like a Snugli or Baby Bjorn) is best. It keeps the infant close for warmth and balances out your backpack. At the same time, though, you must watch for baby overheating in a front pack, so you'll need to remove the infant from your body at rest stops.

Once children reach about 20 pounds, they typically can hold their heads up and sit on their own. At that point, you'll want a baby carrier (sometimes called a child carrier or baby backpack), which can transfer the infant's weight to your hips when you walk. You'll not only be comfortable, but your child will love it, too.

Look for a baby carrier that is sturdy yet lightweight. Your child is going to get heavier as time passes, so about the only way you can counteract this is to reduce the weight of the items you use to carry things. The carrier also should have adjustment points, as you don't want your child to outgrow the carrier too soon. A padded waist belt and padded shoulder straps are necessary for your comfort. The carrier should provide some kind of head and neck support if you're hauling an infant. It also should offer back support for children of all ages, and leg holes should be wide enough so there's no chafing. You want to be able to load your infant without help, so it should be stable enough to stand so when you take it off the child can sit in it for a moment while you get turned around. Stay away from baby carriers with only shoulder straps as you need the waist belt to help shift the child's weight to your hips for more comfortable walking.

Fanny packs

Also known as a belt bag, a fanny pack is virtually a must for anyone with a baby carrier as you can't otherwise carry a backpack. If your significant other is with you, he or she can carry the backpack, of course. Still, the fanny pack also is a good alternative to a backpack in hot weather, as it will reduce back sweat.

If you have only one or two kids on a hike, or if they also are old enough to carry daypacks, your fanny pack need not be large. A mid-size pouch can carry at least 200 cubic inches of supplies, which is more than enough to accommodate all the materials you need. A good fanny pack also has a place to hook canteens to it.

Canteens

Canteens or plastic bottles filled with water are vital for any hike, no matter how short the trail. You'll need to have enough of them to carry about two pints of water per person for every hour of hiking.

Trekking poles

Also known as walking poles or walking sticks, trekking poles are necessary for maintaining stability on uneven or wet surfaces and to help reduce fatigue. The latter makes them useful on even surfaces. By transferring weight to the arms, a trekking pole can reduce stress on knees and lower back, allowing you to maintain a better posture and to go farther.

If an adult with a baby or toddler on your back, you'll primarily want a trekking pole to help you maintain your balance, even if on a flat surface, and to help absorb some of the impact of your step.

Graphite tips provide the best traction. A basket

just above the tip is a good idea so the stick doesn't sink into mud or sand. Angled cork handles are ergonomic and help absorb sweat from your hands so they don't blister. A strap on the handle to wrap around your hand is useful so the stick doesn't slip out. Telescopic poles are a good idea as you can adjust them as needed based on the terrain you're hiking and as kids grow to accommodate their height.

The pole also needs to be sturdy enough to handle rugged terrain, as you don't want a pole that bends when you press it to the ground. Spring-loaded shock absorbers help when heading down a steep incline but aren't necessary. Indeed, for a short walk across flat terrain, the right length stick is about all you need.

Carabiners

Carabiners are metal loops, vaguely shaped like a D, with a sprung or screwed gate. You'll find that hooking a couple of them to your backpack or fanny pack useful in many ways. For example, if you need to dig through a fanny pack, you can hook the strap of your trekking pole to it. Your hat, camera straps, first-aid kit, and a number of other objects also can connect to them. Hook carabiners to your fanny pack or backpack upon purchasing them, so you don't forget them when packing. Small carabiners with sprung gates are inexpensive, but they do have a limited life span of a couple of dozen hikes.

Navigational tools
Paper maps

Paper maps may sound passé in this age of GPS, but you'll find the variety and breadth of view they offer to be useful. During the planning process, a paper map (even if viewing it online), will be far superior to a GPS device. On the hike, you'll also want a backup to GPS. Or like many casual hikers, you may not own GPS at all, which makes paper maps indispensable.

Standard road maps (which includes printed guides and handmade trail maps) show highways and locations of cities and parks. Maps included in guidebooks, printed guides handed out at parks, and those that are hand-drawn tend to be designed like road maps, and often carry the same positives and negatives.

Topographical maps give contour lines and other important details for crossing a landscape. You'll find them invaluable on a hike into the wilds. The contour lines' shape and their spacing on a topo map show the form and steepness of a hill or bluff, unlike the standard road map and most brochures and hand-drawn trail maps. You'll also know if you're in a woods, which is marked in green, or in a clearing, which is marked in white. If you get lost, figuring out where you are and how to get to where you need to be will be much easier with such information.

Satellite photos offer a view from above that is rendered exactly as it would look from an airplane. Thanks to Google and other online services, you can get fairly detailed pictures of the landscape. Such pictures are an excellent resource when researching a hiking trail. Unfortunately, those pictures don't label what a feature is or what it's called, as would a topo map. Unless there's a stream, determining if a feature is a valley bottom or a ridgeline also can be difficult. Like topo maps, satellite photos (most of which were taken by old Russian spy satellites), can be out of date a few years.

GPS

By using satellites, the global positioning system can find your spot on the Earth to within 10 feet. With a GPS device, you can preprogram the trailhead location and mark key turns and landmarks as well as the hike's end point. This mobile map is a powerful technological tool that almost certainly ensures you won't get lost – so long as you've correctly programmed the information. GPS also can calculate travel time and act as a compass, a barometer and altimeter, making such devices virtually obsolete on a hike.

In remote areas, however, reception is spotty at best for GPS, rendering your mobile map worthless. A GPS device also runs on batteries, and there's always a chance they will go dead. Or you may drop your device, breaking it in the process. Their screens are small, and sometimes you need a large paper map to get a good sense of the natural landmarks around you.

Compass

Like a paper map, a compass is indispensable even if you use GPS. Should your GPS no longer function, the compass then can be used to tell you which direction you're heading. A protractor compass is best for hiking. Beneath the compass needle is a transparent base with lines to help your orient yourself. The compass often serves as a magnifying glass to help you make out map details. Most protractor compasses also come with a lanyard for easy carrying.

Food and water

Water

As water is the heaviest item you'll probably carry, there is a temptation to not take as much as one should. Don't skimp on the amount of water you bring, though; after all, it's the one supply your body most needs. It's always better to end up having more water than you needed than returning to your vehicle dehydrated.

How much water should you take? Adults need at least a quart for every two hours hiking. Children need to drink about a quart every two hours of walking and more if the weather is hot or dry. To keep kids hydrated, have them drink at every rest stop.

Don't presume there will be water on the hiking trail. Most trails outside of urban areas lack such amenities. In addition, don't drink water from local streams, lakes, rivers or ponds. There's no way to tell if local water is safe or not. As soon as you have drunk half of your water supply, you should turn around for the vehicle.

Food

Among the many wonderful things about hiking is that snacking between meals isn't frowned upon. Unless going on an all-day hike in which you'll picnic along the way, you want to keep everyone in your hiking party fed, especially as hunger can lead to lethargic and discounted children. It'll also keep young kids from snacking on the local flora or dirt. Before hitting the trail, you'll want to repackage as much of the food as possible as products sold at grocery stores tend to come in bulky packages that take up space and add a little weight to your backpack. Place the food in re-sealable plastic bags.

Bring a variety of small snacks for rest stops. You don't want kids filling up on snacks, but you do need them to maintain their energy levels if they're walking or to ensure they don't turn fussy if riding in a baby carrier. Go for complex carbohydrates and proteins for maintaining energy. Good options include dried fruits, jerky, nuts, peanut butter, prepared energy bars, candy bars with a high protein content (nuts, peanut butter), crackers, raisins and trail mix (called "gorp"). A number of trail mix recipes are available online (*hikeswithtykes.blogspot.com*); you and your children may want to try them out at home to see which ones you collectively like most.

Salty treats rehydrate better than sweet treats do. Chocolate and other sweets are fine if they're not all that's exclusively served, but remember they also tend to lead to thirst and to make sticky messes. Whichever snacks you choose, don't experiment with food on the trail. Bring what you know kids will like.

Give the first snack within a half-hour of leaving the trailhead or you risk children becoming tired and whiny from low energy levels. If kids start asking for them every few steps even after having something to eat at the last rest stop, consider timing snacks to reaching a seeable landmark, such as, "We'll get out the trail mix when we reach that bend up ahead."

Milk for infants

If you have an infant or unweaned toddler with you, milk is as necessary as water. Children who only drink breastfed milk but don't have their mother on the hike require that you have breast-pumped milk in an insulated beverage container (such as a Thermos) that can keep it cool to avoid spoiling. Know how much the child drinks and at what frequency so you can bring enough. You'll also need to carry the child's bottle and feeding nipples. Bring enough extra water in your canteen so you can wash out the bottle after each feeding. A handkerchief can be used to dry bottles between feedings.

Don't forget the baby's pacifier. Make sure it has a string and hook on it so it connects to the baby's outfit and isn't lost.

What not to bring

Avoid soda and other caffeinated beverages, alcohol, and energy pills. The caffeine will dehydrate children as well as you. Alcohol has no place on the trail; you need your full faculties when making decisions and driving home. Energy pills essentially are a stimulant and like alcohol can lead to bad calls. If you're tired, get some sleep and hit the trail another day.

First-aid kit

After water, this is the most essential item you can carry.

A first-aid kit should include:

■ Adhesive bandages of various types and sizes, especially butterfly bandages (for younger kids, make sure they're colorful kid bandages)

■ Aloe vera

- Anesthetic (such as Benzocaine)
- Antacid (tablets)
- Antibacterial (aka antibiotic) ointment (such as Neosporin or Bacitracin)
- Anti-diarrheal tablets (for adults only, as giving this to a child is controversial)
- Anti-itch cream or calamine lotion
- Antiseptics (such as hydrogen peroxide, iodine or Betadine, Mercuroclear, rubbing alcohol)
- Baking soda
- Breakable (or instant) ice packs
- Cotton swabs
- Disposable syringe (w/o needle)
- Epipen (if children or adults have allergies)
- Fingernail clippers (your multi-purpose tool might have this, and if so you can dispense with it)
- Gauze bandage
- Gauze compress pads (2x2 individually wrapped pad)
- Hand sanitizer (use this in place of soap)
- Liquid antihistamine (not Benadryl tablets, however, as children should take liquid not pills; be aware that liquid antihistamines may cause drowsiness)
- Medical tape
- Moisturizer containing an anti-inflammatory
- Mole skin
- Pain reliever (a.k.a. aspirin; for children's pain relief, use liquid acetaminophen such Tylenol or liquid ibuprofen; never give aspirin to a child

under 12)
- Poison ivy cream (for treatment)
- Poison ivy soap
- Powdered sports drinks mix or electrolyte additives
- Sling
- Snakebite kit
- Thermometer
- Tweezers (your multi-purpose tool may have this allowing you to dispense with it)
- Water purification tablets

If infants are with you, be sure to also carry teething ointment (such as Orajel) and diaper rash treatment.

Many of the items should be taken out of their store packaging to make placement in your fanny pack or backpack easier. In addition, small amounts of some items – such as baking soda and cotton swabs – can be placed inside re-sealable plastic bags, since you won't need the whole amount purchased.

Make sure the first-aid items are in a waterproof container. A re-sealable plastic zipper bag is perfectly fine. As Wisconsin is a humid climate, be sure to replace the adhesive bandages every couple of months, as they can deteriorate in the moistness. Also, check your first-aid kit every few trips and after any hike in which you've just used it, so that you can replace used components and to make sure medicines haven't expired.

If you have older elementary-age kids and teen-agers who've been trained in first aid, giving them a kit to carry as well as yourself is a good idea. Should they find themselves lost or if you cannot get to them for a few moments, the kids might need to provide very basic first aid to one another.

Hiking with children: Attitude adjustment

To enjoy hiking with kids, you'll first have to adopt your child's perspective. Simply put, we must learn to hike on our kids' schedules – even though they may not know that's what we're doing.

Compared to adults, kids can't walk as far, they can't walk as fast, and they will grow bored more quickly. Every step we take requires three for them. In addition, early walkers, up to 2 years of age, prefer to wander than to "hike." Preschool kids will start to walk the trail, but at a rate of only about a mile per hour. With stops, that can turn a three-mile hike into a four-hour journey. Kids also won't be able to hike as steep of trails as you or handle as inclement of weather as you might.

This all may sound limiting, especially to long-time backpackers used to racking up miles or bag-ging peaks on their hikes, but it's really not. While you may have to put off some backcountry and mountain climbing trips for a while, it also opens up to you a number of great short trails and nature hikes with spectacular sights that you may have otherwise skipped because they weren't challeng–

ing enough.

So sure, you'll have to make some compromises, but the payout is high. You're not personally on the hike to get a workout but to spend quality time with your children.

Family dog

Dogs are part of the family, and if you have children, they'll want to share the hiking experience with their pets. In turn, dogs will have a blast on the trail, some larger dogs can be used as Sherpas, and others will defend against threatening animals.

But there is a downside to dogs. Many will chase animals and so run the risk of getting lost or injured. Also, a doggy bag will have to be carried for dog pooh – yeah, it's natural, but also inconsiderate to leave for other hikers to smell and for their kids to step in. In addition, most dogs almost always will lose a battle against a threatening animal, so there's a price to be paid for your safety.

Many places where you'll hike solve the dilemma for you as dogs aren't allowed on their trails. Dogs are verboten on some Wisconsin State Parks trails but usually permitted on those in national forests. Always check with the park ranger before heading to the trail.

If you can bring a dog, make sure it is well behaved and friendly to others. You don't need your dog biting another hiker while unnecessarily defending its family.

Rules of the trail

Ah, the woods or a wide open meadow, peaceful and quiet, not a single soul around for miles. Now you and your children can do whatever you want.

Not so fast.

Act like wild animals on a hike, and you'll destroy the very aspects of the wilds that make them so attractive. Act like wild animals, and you're likely to end up back in civilization, specifically an emergency room. And there are other people around. Just as you would wish them to treat you courteously, so you and your children should do the same for them.

Let's cover how to act civilized out in the wilds.

Minimize damage to your surroundings

When on the trail, follow the maxim of "Leave no trace." Obviously, you shouldn't toss litter on the ground, start rockslides, or pollute water supplies. How much is damage and how much is good-natured exploring is a gray area, of course. Most serious backpackers will say you should never pick up objects, break branches, throw rocks, pick flowers, and so on – the idea is not to disturb the environment at all.

Good luck getting a four-year-old to think like that. The good news is a four-year-old won't be able to throw around many rocks or break many branches.

Still, children from their first hike into the wilderness should be taught to respect nature and to not destroy their environment. While you might overlook a preschooler hurling rocks into a puddle, they can be taught to sniff rather than pick flowers. As they grow older, you can teach them the value of leaving the rock alone. Regardless of age, don't allow children to write on boulders or carve into trees.

Many hikers split over picking berries. To strictly abide by the "minimize damage" principle, you wouldn't pick any berries at all. Kids, however, are likely to find great pleasure in eating black-berries, currants, and thimbleberries as ambling down the trail. Personally, I don't see any probably enjoying a few berries if the long-term payoff is a respect and love for nature. To minimize damage, teach them to only pick berries they can reach from the trail so they don't trample plants or deplete food supplies for animals. They also should only pick what they'll eat.

Collecting is another issue. In national and most state and county parks, taking rocks, flower blossoms and even pine cones is illegal. Picking flowers moves many species, especially if they are rare and native, one step closer to extinction. Archeological ruins are extremely fragile, and even touching them can damage a site.

But on many trails, especially gem trails, collecting is part of the adventure. Use common sense – if the point of the trail is to find materials to collect, such as a gem trail, take judiciously, meaning don't overcollect. Otherwise, leave it there.

Sometimes the trail crosses private land. If so, walking around fields, not through them, always is best or you could damage a farmer's crops.

Pack out what you pack in

Set the example as a parent: Don't litter yourself; whenever stopping, pick up whatever you've dropped; and always require kids to pick up after themselves when they litter. In the spirit of "Leave no trace," try to leave the trail cleaner than you found it, so if you come across litter that's safe to pick up, do so and bring it back to a trash bin in civilization. Given this, you may want to bring a plastic bag to carry out garbage.

Picking up litter doesn't just mean gum and candy wrappers but also some organic materials that take a long time to decompose and aren't likely to be part of the natural environment you're hiking. In particular, these include peanuts shells, orange peelings, and eggshells.

Burying litter, by the way, isn't viable. Either animals or erosion soon will dig it up, leaving it scattered around the trail and woods.

Stay on the trail

Hiking off trail means potentially damaging fragile growth. Following this rule not only ensures you minimize damage but is also a matter of safety. Off trail is where kids most likely will encounter dangerous animals and poisonous plants. Not being able to see where they're stepping also increases the likelihood of falling and injuring themselves. Leaving the trail raises the chances of getting lost. Staying on the trail also means staying out of caves, mines or abandoned structures you may encounter. They are usually dangerous places.

Finally, never let children take a shortcut on a switchback trail. Besides putting them on steep ground upon which they could slip, their impatient act will cause the switchback to erode.

Trail dangers

On Wisconsin trails, two common dangers face hikers: ticks and poison ivy/sumac. Both can make your stay at the cabin or your time once back home miserable. Fortunately, both threats are easily avoidable and treatable.

Ticks

One of the greatest dangers comes from the smallest of creatures: ticks. Both the wood and the deer tick are common in the state, and can infect people with Lyme disease and much more rarely Rocky Mountain spotted fever.

Ticks usually leap onto people from the top of a grass blade as you brush against it, so walking in the middle of the trail away from high plants is a good idea. Wearing a hat, a long sleeve shirt tucked into pants, and pants tucked into shoes or socks, also will keep ticks off you, though this is not foolproof as they sometimes can hook onto clothing. A tightly woven cloth provides the best protection, however. Children can pick up a tick that has hitchhiked onto the family dog, so outfit Rover and Queenie with a tick-repelling collar.

After hiking into an area where ticks live, you'll want to examine your children's bodies (as well as your own) for them. Check warm, moist areas of the skin, such as under the arms, the groin and head hair. Wearing light-colored clothing helps make the tiny tick easier to spot.

To get rid of a tick that has bitten your child, drip either disinfectant or rubbing alcohol on the bug, so it will loosen its grip. Grip the tick close to its head, slowly pulling it away from the skin. This hopefully will prevent it from releasing saliva that spreads disease. Rather than kill the tick, keep it in a plastic bag so that medical professionals can analyze it should disease symptoms appear. Next, wash the bite area with soap and water then apply antiseptic.

In the days after leaving the woods, also check for signs of disease from ticks. Look for bulls-eye rings, a sign of a Lyme disease. Other symptoms include a large red rash, joint pain, and flu-like symptoms. Indications of Rocky Mountain spotted fever include headache, fever, severe muscle aches, and a spotty rash first on palms and feet soles that spread, all beginning about two days after the bite.

If any of these symptoms appear, seek medical attention immediately. Fortunately, antibiotics exist to cure most tick-related diseases.

Poison ivy/sumac

Often the greatest danger in the wilds isn't our own clumsiness or foolhardiness but various plants we encounter. The good news is that we mostly have to force the encounter with flora. Touching the leaves of either poison ivy or poison sumac in particular results in an itchy, painful rash. Each plant's sticky resin, which causes the reaction, clings to clothing and hair, so you may not have "touched" a leaf, but once your hand runs against the resin on shirt or jeans, you'll probably get the rash.

To avoid touching these plants, you'll need to be able to identify each one. Remember the "Leaves of three, let it be" rule for poison ivy. Besides groups of three leaflets, poison ivy has shiny green leaves that are red in spring and fall. Poison sumac's leaves are not toothed as are non-poisonous sumac, and in autumn their leaves turn scarlet. Be forewarned that even after leaves fall off, poison oak's stems can carry some of the itchy resin.

By staying on the trail and walking down its middle rather than the edges, you are unlikely to come into contact with this pair of irritating plants. That probably is the best preventative. Poison ivy barrier creams also can be helpful, but they only temporarily block the resin. This lulls you into a false sense of safety, and so you may not bother to watch for poison ivy.

To treat poison ivy/sumac, wash the part of the body that has touched the plant with poison ivy soap and cold water. This will erode the oily resin, so it'll be easier to rinse off. If you don't have any of this special soap, plain soap sometimes will work if used within a half-hour of touching the plant. Apply a poison ivy cream and get medical attention immediately. Wearing gloves, remove any clothing (including shoes) that has touched the plants, washing them and the worn gloves right away.

For more about these topics and many others, pick up this author's "Hikes with Tykes: A Practical Guide to Day Hiking with Kids." You also can find tips online at the author's "Hikes with Tykes" blog (*hikeswithtykes.blogspot.com*). Have fun on the trail!

Featured Trails

From awe-inspiring beaches along Lake Superior to quaint walks past picturesque dairy farms, from some of the tallest waterfalls east of the Rockies to unique, disappearing ecosystems, from 1.2-billion year-old lava rock to ponds formed just a few thousand years ago, northwest Wisconsin offers an incredible number of sights for day hikers to enjoy. During the pages ahead, we'll look in-depth at the most impressive trails in each of the region's most visited communities and offer lists of other great nearby trails you'll want to hit during your stay.

Amery

Stower Seven Lakes State Trail

Peaceful woodland, serene ponds, and comely farms await day hikers on the Stower Seven Lakes State Trail heading west of Amery.

Built on a former rail line, the 14-mile trail heads to a mile short of Dresser. A good segment to take is from the trailhead in Amery for about 3 miles to the southern tip of Bear Trap Lake.

With a surface of crushed limestone and the generally level grade of rail lines (To save locomotive fuel consumption, railroads sought grades of no more than 3 percent for their lines.), the trail is easy for families with children to handle. Mile post signs conveniently punctuate the trail.

In Amery, the trail begins on Harriman Avenue west of State Hwy. 46. A public parking lot is near the trail just east of Harriman Avenue.

About 0.2 miles in as leaving Amery, the trail crosses between the North Twin and South Twin lakes. On North Twin Lake, a popular fishing destination, watch for bald eagles diving to snare walleye or Northern pike for a meal. Loons also can be spotted here.

At just under a mile, the trail crosses Baker Avenue. Though the area is moderately built up, the trail is nicely wooded with maple and oak, keeping you isolated from the sights of modern life.

Around 1.5 miles, the trail skirts a small group of

ponds to the north. After that, farmland is visible between the tree breaks to the north and soon becomes more prevalent.

The trail is named for Harvey and Marilyn Stower of Amery. For many years, Harvey served in the Wisconsin Legislature and as Amery's mayor.

As nearing Deronda, the trail intersects a couple of highways, so be safe when crossing them.

The first of them comes at about 2.5 miles, when the trail junctions with State Hwy. 115. The next comes at about 2.8 miles with County Road F.

About three miles in, the trail reaches the southern tip of Bear Trap Lake with Kinney Lake to the south. This marks a good spot to turn around.

If time and energy permits, though, continue onward. At Deronda, the trail heads three more miles to Wanderoos, then five miles to Nye, and finally 2.5 miles to its end at 90th Avenue near Dresser.

Nearby Trails

■ **Amery Regional Medical Center Walking Trail** – The local hospital grounds provides a community walking path running along the Apple River. The forested path nicely keeps views of the urban area to a minimum.

■ **Cattail State Trail** – A plethora of scenery from woodlands to rolling pastures awaits hikers on this 18-mile trail that runs to Turtle Lake. From the Amery end, the trail begins in woodland then passes through farmland and prairie.

■ **Green Trail** – North of the city, a hat trick of trails at the Balsam Branch Cross Country Ski Trails make their way through woodlands for hiking, skiing and snowshoeing. Try the Green Trail, a 3-mile trail that includes a segment circling a pond with swans.

■ **York Park Walking Trail** – Three miles of graveled trails take hikers through a hardwood forest and past a lakeshore in this 40-acre park. Despite the park's urban setting, it's a prime location to spot a variety of birds, including common loons, bald eagles and osprey.

■ **Also see:** *Balsam Lake, Clear Lake, Osceola, St. Croix Falls, Turtle Lake*

Ashland

Morgan Falls St. Peter's Dome Trail
Chequamegon National Forest

An 80-foot waterfall and impressive vista with views 20 miles around await cabin-goers near Ashland.

The Morgan Falls St. Peter's Dome Trail in the Chequamegon (pronounced SHO-WAH-MA-GON) National Forest actually can be broken into two trails depending on your time and energy. The first 0.6 miles of the trail heads to Morgan Falls (for a 1.2 mile round trip), or you can continue another 1.2 miles to the top of St. Peter's Dome (for a 3.6-mile round trip). Late spring to early fall is the best time to walk the trail.

To reach the trailhead, take Hwy. 63 about 22 miles north of Cable. Turn east onto County Road E, driving six miles to the Ashland-Bayfield Road (aka Forest Road 199). Turn south. It's 4.2 miles to the parking lot. Watch for the trailhead sign at the parking lot.

Either a day pass ($5) or an annual forest pass ($20) is needed to travel to the trailhead (as is required throughout the Chequamegon).

The first portion of the trail is fairly flat and graveled and even accessible for people with disabilities. After a half-mile walk through a wooded area, Morgan Falls – Wisconsin's second highest waterfall – comes into view. The water zigzags some dozen feet down a rock face before splashing into a small pool. It overflows the pool falling another eight feet in different streams down a crooked granite cliff to the bottom in an intimate setting.

Be forewarned: During drought years, the water flow can be a little better than a trickle.

If continuing on to St. Peters Dome, the trail gets a little more rugged, becoming a dirt path cutting over roots and stones across shallow creeks. The autumn colors are impressive, and in spring wildflowers including the large-flowered trillium, violets and Dutchman's-breeches dot the undergrowth and trail sides.

Other sites are located on the way. Among them is a circular stone cistern built at an abandoned

Civilian Conservation Corps campground constructed during the 1930s. A stone quarry from the mid-20th century (red granite is used to make countertops) also exists; it also is no longer in operation.

A number of rare ferns are situated along the trail. Among them are Braun's hollyfern, woodfern, and northern maidenhair fern. Hemlock and Canada yew also abound in large patches.

The trail does become steep as ascending St. Peter's Dome, which sits at 1,565 feet elevation.

From atop this ancient formation of red granite, Chequamagon Bay in Lake Superior at 20 miles away is visible on clear and dry days. With binoculars, you also might be able to spot the Michigan Island lighthouse, about 33 miles away, if you look northeast through a gap in the trees.

The vista is a massive red granite dome that began to form some 1.2 billion years ago. Magma crystallized underground, mixing with quartz and feldspar, which gives the granite a pink to orange coloring. Weathering over the eons has brought the granite "above" ground.

From the dome top, take the same route back to the trailhead.

Nearby Trails
■ **Interpretive Boardwalk Trail** – At the Northern Great Lakes Visitor Center west of town, a 0.75-mile trail wends its way through three coastal wet-

land ecosystems: a black ash swamp, a sedge meadow, and a cedar and tamarack swamp. If you have children, be sure to stop at the visitor center, where they can crawl through a beaver lodge and engage in other fun (but educational!) activities.

■ **Tri-County Corridor Trail** – On its way to Superior, the trail runs west out of town. A pastoral segment is between Pine Creek Road and County Road G. Park at the Moquah Town Hall and head east for a 1-mile round trip.

■ **Waterfront Trail** – This 10-mile trail loops around Ashland, passing through several parks and a beach along the way. A scenic segment runs along the Lake Superior shoreline from Maslowski Beach to Howard Pearson Plaza for about two miles one way.

■ **Also see:** *Bayfield, Drummond, Iron River, Mellen, Washburn*

Balsam Lake

Blue Trail
Balsam Branch Cross Country Ski Trails

Cabin-goers can truly get back to nature by hiking the Blue Trail of Balsam Branch Cross Country Ski Trails.

Located south of Balsam Lake but conveniently close to the nearby towns of St. Croix Falls and Amery, Balsam Branch's trails can be used for day hiking once the snow disappears. The area is virtually all forested with Northern hardwoods and so is quite beautiful in autumn when leaves change color.

The trails cross three recreational areas – the D.D. Kennedy Environmental Area, Lake Wapogasset Bible Camp, and the Garfield Recreation Area. Nordic Ski Club of Amery manages the trails in winter.

The ski trails consist of a number of meandering loops of varying lengths and grades. Of the three general trails that the loops break into, the Blue Trail sits in middle as far as difficulty is concerned.

To reach the trail, from U.S. Hwy. 8 in Polk County turn south onto 150th Street then east onto 120th Avenue. East of Kennedy Mill Avenue, take the next right to the parking lot.

From the lot, head straight south for 0.37 miles. You'll notice right away that the trail is nicely shaded. Maple and oak predominate, but as the terrain closes on lower-lying, wetter areas in Balsam Branch, you'll see birch and tamarack.

At the first junction, go left for 0.12 miles, beneath a power line. Large and small game abound along the trails. You're very likely to spot white-tailed deer here, as well as squirrels, chipmunks and rabbits.

Upon reaching the next trail junction, go right, then wind south and west for 0.68 miles. At the next tee intersection, go left for 0.5 miles.

As recent as 12,000 BC, Balsam Branch sat under

the leading edge of a massive glacier. As the glacier melted and retreated, outwash covered this region.

At the next trail junction, beneath the power line, go right/north for 0.25 miles. Many of the boulders and stones covering the ground in this area were carried and left here by that glacier.

Upon reaching the next trail junction, the route rejoins the Green Trail; go left for 0.19 miles. At the tee intersection, go right for 0.25 miles to the parking lot.

The Blue Trail runs about 2.36 miles. Different loops and connectors (see below) can be combined to add to the trail length.

Nearby Trails

■ **Black Trail** – This 3.4-mile trail is among the Balsam Branch Cross Country Ski Trails and passes Ox Lake and a couple of ponds as winding its way through a hardwood forest in the Lake Wapogasset Bible Camp, and the Garfield Recreation Area. The paths are wide.

■ **D.D. Kennedy Environmental Area trails** – The 1.25 miles of unnamed trails west of the Balsam Branch Cross Country Ski Trails form two loops. Part of one loop circles Balsam Branch River, where the waterway widens into a lake, and includes two foot-bridges.

■ **Also see:** *Amery, Cumberland, Frederic/Luck, St. Croix Falls, Turtle Lake*

Bayfield
Bay View Trail, Boardwalk, nature trail
Big Bay State Park

Incredible views of Lake Superior await hikers traveling to Big Bay State Park in the northern tip of Wisconsin.

The park sits on Madeline Island, the largest of the famous 22 Apostle Islands. Taking the Bay View Trail along with a boardwalk and a self-guided interpretive trail afford hikers a 5-mile round trip, though this can be cut in half if turning around at the boardwalk.

To avoid the Northwoods cold, visit in June and July. You'll have to first load your vehicle aboard the Madeline Island Ferry, which runs every half hour from Bayport on the mainland to La Pointe on the island. After a 20-minute ride across the lake, take County Road H east for about four miles. Turn right/east on Hagen Road. The park entrance is in 2 miles; you'll need to pay an entry fee.

Continue on the park entry road (aka Haines road), turning right onto Wilderness Road. Where the road loops is a parking lot. The trailhead is on the lot's east side.

An easy, well-maintained trail, you'll pass Point Picnic Area to the edge of Madeline Island. At one time, the island – as well as the other Apostle Islands – was part of the mainland. Four sets of glaciers during the past 100,000 years and the ensuing lakes have eroded the 600 million-year-old sedimentary rock that forms the islands.

Sunsets and glaciers

At the tee intersection with Lake Superior before you, go left onto Bay View Trail (to the right is Point Trail). The wooded trail hugs the shoreline. You're certain to spot wildlife and likely will see some bluff caves. If staying overnight, do the trail at sunset – you won't be disappointed by the spectacular views over Lake Superior's Big Bay.

The largest of the Great Lakes sits atop hard basalt that formed 1.1 billion years ago when the North American continent literally was splitting. Eventually this separation stopped, and the rift filled with sediment. Glaciers during the last Ice Age excavated this sediment and left the cold water that forms the lake.

As rounding the shoreline, Bay View Trail turns into Lagoon Ridge Trail; follow this for a few yards to the boardwalk. If short on time or tired, you may want to turn back here. If the day is young and you're full of energy, go right, continuing along the boardwalk, which cuts through a white and red pine forest sitting upon Big Bay Sand Spit. Bearberry and wintergreen grows beneath the pines.

Nicely flat, the half-mile boardwalk offers benches for resting, interpretive sings and more impressive lake views. A lagoon sits to the boardwalk's left.

Barrier beach

Some 15,000 years ago when Madeline Island reappeared as the glaciers retreated and melted, the lagoon was part of Big Bay. Since then, wave action and lake currents built a pair of barrier beaches, creating the lagoon.

The boardwalk turns into the self-guided nature trail that runs up the spit. You may want to take a break along the beach for a swim.

The nature trail includes a couple of small loops in it. Watch for bald eagles that nest and raise their younglings in the park. Upon reaching the trail's end, turn around and return way you came.

Before coming to the island, make sure you bring insect repellent. Bugs can be bothersome in the trail's forested sections, and repellant sometimes can be difficult to find on the island.

Lakeshore Trail
Apostle Islands National Lakeshore

Cabin-goers don't have to leave the mainland to experience the beauty of the famous Apostle Islands National Lakeshore. A fairly new route, the Lakeshore Trail, runs through a Lake Superior forest, over an impressive sandstone cave formation, and along a windswept beach.

To reach Lakeshore Trail, take State Hwy. 13 to or from Bayfield. At Park Road, turn toward Meyers Beach. A large paved parking lot sits 0.4 miles away at the road's end.

For the trailhead, look for trail signs on the parking lot's northeast side. You'll head east through aspen, birch, several maple varieties, and a few pines. Given the mix of trees and their different fall leaf colors, early September is an ideal time for the hike; mosquitoes also will be few at that time of the year.

A few hundred yards from the parking lot, the trail goes up and down a gully, which in spring and early summer can boast running water. Stepping stones make for an easy fording, though. When you cross a sand road, you're about 0.8 miles along the trail. Continue that same distance again, and you'll begin to glimpse the lake and the trail's highlight: the Mawikwe Bay sea caves.

The lakes' crashing waves and millennia of winter ice carved out honeycombed caves and a 50-foot chasm that runs more than 200 feet long. A natural bridge runs over the formation. The tinted sandstone and rainbows from the spray gives the formation a magical feel.

The caves can't be accessed from the trail except during winter when the lake freezes (You may see kayakers at other times of the year clambering about the caves, however.). During winter, icicles hanging from the sandstone roofs appear otherworldly.

The trail skirts the chasm. If children are with you, make sure they stay away from the cliff edges and off the natural bridge. All are unstable due to constant erosion.

This marks a good place to turn back for a round-trip hike that is slightly more than three miles long. For a more ambitious hike, however, continue onward. After more than a mile on the bluff overlooking the caves, follow the trail inland through the forest. The flat trail winds through more hardwoods in a very peaceful setting.

Be forewarned that once in the forest, the trail can be difficult to follow. Fortunately, it soon meets a dirt road. Turn left onto the road, which drops about 80 feet in elevation, until reaching a sandy beach.

Seagulls are numerous here. The clump of tress across the lake's horizon is Eagle Island. Keep walking east and north along the shoreline for about a half mile or once it turns to cobble. Return the way you came for a roughly 10-mile round trip.

Though the trail is managed by the National Park Service, there is no fee for hikers to enter or park.

Nearby Trails

■ **Big Ravine Trail** – The in-city trail heads for a 2-mile round trip along a steep ravine lined with old-growth hemlocks. You'll find the trailhead at the Sweeney Avenue baseball field behind the outfield fence.

■ **Big Sand Bay Walking Trails** – Paths cut across pine barrens on the Bayfield Peninsula northwest of town. The trails are on the west side of Old County

Highway K Road, about 1.5 miles north of the State Hwy. 13 junction.

■ **Brownstone Trail** – South of town, an old railroad bed converted into a hiking trail makes for a scenic 5-mile round trip hike. The trail passes a marina and offers great views of Madeline Island and sailboats on Lake Superior.

■ **Iron Bridge Nature Hiking Trail** – Also known as the Gil Larsen Trail, the 0.75-mile trail follows a ravine creek under an old iron bridge to an overlook. Pick up the trail in Bayfield on Washington Avenue uphill from the ferry boat landing.

■ **Jerry Jolly Hiking Trail** – The trail winds through the Bayfield County Forest and Nourse Sugarbush State Natural Area. Follow County Highway J/Star Route to the trailhead.

■ **Lost Creek Falls Walking Trail** – Located south of Cornucopia on the peninsula's west side, the trail heads for less than mile one way through pine barrens to Lost Creek. The trailhead is at the end of Trail Road off of County Road C.

■ **Mt. Ashwabay Ski Area hiking trails** – Several ski trails in winter turn to day hiking trails of varying lengths in summer. The ski area is located on Ski Hill Road south of Bayfield.

■ **Pikes Creek Hiking Trail** – The 2-mile round trip trail heads along Pikes Creek and past the state fish hatchery, which boasts two large ponds. Fish species native to Lake Superior are raised there.

■ **Raspberry River Walking Trail** – Northwest of Red Cliff, the trail heads through pine barrens to the Raspberry River, which ultimately flows into Lake Superior. The trailhead is at the intersection of Old County Highway K Road and Rowley Road.

■ **Spring Creek Walking Trails** – About 3.5 miles south of Cornucopia on County Road C, a set of trails run through the pine barrens near the Siskiwit River and lakes. Look on the road's east side for the trailhead.

■ **Sioux River Flats Beach Trail** – For a great beach walk, try this 1.9-mile stretch south of Bayfield. From State Hwy. 13, take Bayview Park Road to a parking area and follow the beach to the Sioux River.

■ **Also see:** *Ashland, Iron River, Washburn*

Birchwood

Tuscobia Trail segment

Wisconsin has nicely converted a number of abandoned railroad grades to hiking and multi-use trails. Among the more popular is the 74-mile Tuscobia Trail running from Rice Lake to Park Falls.

In the southeast corner of Washburn County, the trail passes through the village of Birchwood, the self-proclaimed Bluegill Capital of Wisconsin. A pleasant segment of the trail to day hike goes northeast from downtown Birchwood for a 4-mile round trip to County Road F and back.

Hiking the trail anytime in summer and autumn will prove enjoyable. Note that the trail closes from Nov. 15-Dec. 15 for deer hunting season.

To reach the trail segment, park downtown, picking up the Tuscobia on County Road D/Euclid Avenue just north of the State Hwy. 48 intersection.

After walking just a tenth of a mile, hikers will come to the south end of Birchwood Lake. The popular fishing lake covers 364 acres and is home to largemouth and smallmouth bass, Northern pike, walleye and panfish.

Passing the lake, the trail swerves to the south side of Hwy. 48; be careful when crossing the highway, especially of vehicles turning off La Pointe Drive onto Hwy. 48 a few feet to the east. ATVs also can use the trail, and while it's plenty wide for both vehicle and hiker, always exercise caution.

Construction of the Omaha rail line that is now the Tuscobia begin in 1899 and lasted for some 15 years. By the 1940s when logging was no longer viable in the region, the rail line saw much less usage and eventually ended altogether. Bridges over some waterways were removed in 1967, and the following year locals across the region began a long effort to convert it to a hiking trail.

Upon leaving town, the trail passes scenic farmland. Trees line the walking path, offering some shade.

Amid the scenery, you'll cross an invisible boundary into Rusk County then enter a bucolic woods of mixed hardwoods.

Upon reaching County Road F, you've gone two miles. This marks a good spot to turn around, though the trail does continue for several more miles on its way to Couderay.

Nearby Trails

■ **Ice Age National Scenic Trail segment** – Directly south of town, the Ice Age Trail cuts roughly north-south through the Cedar Lake Area County Forest. Take the forest's easternmost jeep trail off Lemler Lane and pick up the Ice Age Trail for a 3.5-mile walk one way to Pigeon Creek.

■ **Red Oak East and West trails** – Located northwest of town at the Hunt Hill Audubon Sanctuary, combine the two looping trails for a 1.8-mile hike. Despite the trails' names, the highlight is a grove of large white pines that have been growing since the 1800s.

■ **Also see:** *Hayward, Rice Lake, Shell Lake/Sarona, Spooner*

Cable

Forest Lodge Nature Trail
Chequamegon National Forest

Among the best hikes to learn about the Wisconsin Northwoods is the Forest Lodge Nature Trail, east of Cable in southern Bayfield County. Located in the Chequamegon National Forest, the 1.5-mile loop is maintained in cooperation with the Cable Natural History Museum.

Any dry summer day is an excellent day to hike the trail, and fall colors are spectacular with trees usually remaining golden until the third week in October.

To reach the trail, take County Road M for about 8.6 miles east of Cable. Turn left/north on Garmish Road. The parking lot/trailhead is a mile later on the road's right/south side. A forest pass is required to park.

From the lot, head straight south into an old field. If you turn left, you'll end up on the neighboring Conservancy Trail.

While fairly flat, the trail does narrow from four- to two-feet wide upon reaching the woods. The forested section of the trail sports some rough tread as well.

The trail rambles through a number of ecosystems, offering a mini-walk through the region's natural history.

Among the ecosystems is a lowland bog, surrounded by spruce and slender-stemmed cotton grass. Here you'll also find the carnivorous bog-dwelling pitcher plant.

Another ecosystem – now rare for northern Wisconsin – is of old-growth white pines. During the 1880s when pioneers settled the area, the white pine dominated; after being logged off, hardwoods replaced them.

A good portion of the trail is that newer upland hardwood forest. Chipmunks are abundant here.

One element of the landscape hasn't changed, though: glacial erratics. These are boulders and rocks brought here during the last ice age that are different in color and composition than those "native" to the area.

Hikers also will walk through a grove of hemlocks, which looks like a scene out of a fairy tale, and an experimental prairie.

An excellent way to identify and learn more about these sights is the interpretive booklet available at the Cable Natural History Museum, located in Cable at 13470 County Highway M.

Nearby Trails

■ **Birkebeiner Trail** – Known primarily for the annual ski race held on the trail, the Birkie also makes a great hiking route in summer and can be accessed at either the Telemark Resort or the North End Cabin. Hikers don't need a pass for the trail.

■ **Namekagon Trail East Loop** – Located northeast of town in the Chequamegon National Forest, the 1-mile East Loop of this three-loop trail can be hiked in summer. You're very likely to hear and possibly even spot Northwoods wildlife along the walk.

■ **North End Trail** – South of town, this ski trail in winter is often day hiked the other seasons. Consisting of several crisscrossing routes, combine the

Ridge and Bear Paw loops for a 1.6-mile walk.

■ **Rock Lake Trail** – Narrow loops of varying lengths run through the Chequamegon around Rock, Frels and Hildebrand lakes. Hiking is best on the segments running from Forest Road 207 to any of these lakes.

■ **Also see:** *Clam Lake/Glidden, Drummond, Hayward*

Cameron/Chetek

Moose Ear Creek Trail

Moose Ear Creek/Sumner Area County Forest

Hikers on the Moose Ear Creek Trail in the Cameron-Chetek area may want to bring bait and tackle. A walk alongside the stream is certain to bring back thoughts of those Ernest Hemingway trout-fishing days of old.

Located in the Moose Ear Creek/Sumner Area County Forest, the trail runs roughly two miles out and back. It's lush with vegetation in summer, vibrant with colors in autumn, and gurgling with fast-flowing snowmelt in spring.

To reach the trailhead, from Cameron head east on U.S. Hwy. 8. Turn right in the Barron County forest's eastern-most entrance just before reaching Moose Ear Creek. Park at the head of the forest trail immediately beyond the high wire lines.

From the lot, the trail heads southward. Don't

worry about the gate; it's merely there to prevent vehicle traffic.

You'll walk southwest for roughly 0.35 miles. At the forest road junction, go left/east. A good mix of Northern hardwoods line the trail.

At 0.125 miles, the trail comes to a spur leading to Moose Ear Creek. A Class I trout stream, Moose Ear Creek begins as a rock-bottomed brook in the Blue Hills to the north. The hills are all that remain of an ancient mountain range. Glaciers just 10,000 years ago ground the then low mountains to their current heights.

Today, the creek flowing out of the Blue Hills is an excellent brook and brown trout stream. Bird watching is superb as well; keep an eye out for the golden-winged warbler, Louisiana waterthrush, red-shouldered hawk, and whip-poor-will.

Continuing south, the trail parallels the stream. After about 0.4 miles, the trail swerves away from the creek, which flows south into Moose Ear Lake, a 33.6-acre waterbody sporting a warm water fish population.

Upon coming to next trail junction, you've hiked about a mile. This marks a good spot to turn back.

Nearby Trails

■ **Chetek Area County Forest trails**– On 11th Avenue, take the second gated jeep trail heading west to a fire tower for a 0.6-mile round trip hike.

■ **Pioneer Village Museum** – Take a walk back

through time at the Barron County Historical Society's living history museum in Cameron. Events usually are scheduled on weekends; admission is charged.

■ **Veterans Memorial Park trails** – Southeast of Cameron, short trails run through a wooded area alongside Prairie Lake. The park, which includes several public amenities, stretches across 160 acres.

■ **Also see:** *Rice Lake*

Clam Lake/Glidden
West Torch Trail
Chequamegon National Forest

Hikers can escape modern life into a thick, serene woods on the West Torch Trail south of Clam Lake in the Chequamegon National Forest.

Wild Torch is a stacked loop trail system with loop lengths of 0.8, 1.7, 3.7, and 5 miles. The longer two loops offer some hilly terrain, but combining the 0.8 and 1.7 loops makes for an easy 2.2-mile hike (The loops share a stretch of trail.).

To reach the trailhead, from Clam Lake take County Road GG south for 2.5 miles. The parking lot is located on the road's left/east side.

From the lot, go left/northeast to do the trail clockwise. This is opposite of the way cross country skiers would do the trail in winter. The terrain is mainly flat with a few gentle rolls.

About 0.15 miles in, you'll reach a trail junction; keep going straight (Going left takes you on the longest of the four looping trails.). Trees nicely shade the entire walking path, which are narrower than jeep trails but wider than most in the back-country. Species lining the route are common to the Chequamegon and include pines, aspens, oak, paper birch, and sugar maple.

Upon reaching the next trail junction, about 0.15 miles later, continue straight/northeast. From there, the trail curves south and then east. Watch the ground for a number of different wildflowers that blossom through the year. Common blooms in the region include the downy yellow violet, the large-flowered bellwort, the large-flowered trillium, and the wood anemone.

Continue right/south at the next trail junction (If going straight, you'll end up on the third longest of the loops.). Red squirrels particularly like this section of the forest, but don't be surprised if you spot other woodland animals, including white-tailed deer, chipmunks and rabbits. A variety of small birds also fill the air with song through the day.

At the next trail junction, go right/west. You'll pass one more junction, at which you would go straight/left back to the parking lot.

A final note that while hiking the trail is free, a recreation pass is required for parking anywhere in the Chequamegon.

Nearby Trails

■ **Ashland County Forest hunter walking trails** – Several walking trails for hunters as well as jeep trails crisscross the 40,000-acre Ashland County Forest near Glidden and Butternut. Wildlife is abundant in the forest; watch for signs of black bears.

■ **Little Pelican Lake Trail** – In the Flambeau River State Forest south of these two communities, a short trail loops through the woods west of Little Pelican Lake. The trailhead is in a parking lot off of Snuss Boulevard immediately south of the State Hwy. 70 junction.

■ **Also see:** *Ashland, Cable, Drummond, Hayward, Mellen*

Clear Lake

Clear Lake-Clayton State Trail

Eleven miles of old rail bed have been converted into a walking path running between the two Polk County villages of Clear Lake and Clayton, the trail's namesakes. The trail passes several lakes as it nears Clayton.

A good segment of the Clear Lake-Clayton Trail to hike during summer is a 3-mile round trip west of Clayton from County Road P to 65th Avenue.

Park at the public boat landing for Magnor Lake on U.S. Hwy. 63 west of Clayton. Magnor Lake covers 229 acres and at 26 feet deep is a popular spot for catching panfish, largemouth bass, Northern pike and walleye. The lake's water clarity is low, though.

To reach the trailhead, you'll have to cross Hwy. 63 as the trail is on the south/east side of that road. Exercise caution as crossing and watch for traffic turning off of County Road P onto Hwy. 63.

The fairly flat and wide trail parallels Hwy. 63, but a good mix of hardwood trees and bushes line both sides of the path, keeping out the views of passing traffic and offering moderate shade. The trail is popular among ATVs, but there's plenty of room for both three-wheelers and walkers.

Heading south from Magnor Lake, you'll enter farm country with fields visible through the tree breaks on both sides of the trail.

At not quite half way to your turn-back point, you'll catch sight of Barbo Lake, also on your right. Though shallow at only four-feet deep, it covers 43.5 acres.

From there, the trail curves southward. Near the turn-back point, you'll likely spot Paulson Lake between the trees on the right. At 25 acres and 12 feet deep, the lake sports panfish, largemouth bass and Northern pike.

Upon reaching 65th Avenue, you've gone 1.5 miles. This marks a good spot to head back.

Nearby Trails
■**Cattail State Trail** – North of town, pick up the

state trail that runs between Amery and Almena. Crushed stone covers the route, and the old rail line is smooth with the most gradual of elevation gains.

■ **Clear Lake Village Park** – A short trail takes hikers through tall oaks and white-barked birch trees to French Lake. In autumn, an array of colors from the variety of trees in the 260-acre park are impressive.

■ **Also see:** *Amery, Turtle Lake, Somerset*

Cumberland
Ice Age National Scenic Trail segment

North of Cumberland, a fairly flat segment of the expansive Ice Age National Scenic Trail runs at the edge of where the glacier last seen in these parts towered some 10,000 years ago. The hike to Grassy Lake and back makes for just under four miles round trip.

To reach the trail, from Cumberland drive north on U.S. Hwy. 63 into Washburn County. At Brick Yard Road, go right/east. At the next intersection, turn right/south onto Old Hwy. 63; park off this road across from the Pershing Road intersection.

The trail unofficially heads east alongside Pershing Road. You'll pass bucolic farm fields at first, but the trail grows increasingly forested as heading east. Typical Northern hardwoods – maples and oaks – with scattered pines line the route.

At about 0.75 miles, the trail turns left/north. This now official segment of the Ice Age Trail runs on public land. If you feel uncomfortable leaving your car along the highway or want to shorten your walk, this is a good alternative for parking (Though it'll still have to be on the roadside.).

Some 10,000 years ago, this area was beneath a towering glacier, only miles away from its leading edge to the south. The glacier crushed and flattened the landscape, and remnants of it formed many of the lakes seen across northern Wisconsin by depressing the land and melting. The trail largely traces the extent of the glacier during the most recent ice age.

For the next 1.25 miles, the trail roughly parallels the shoreline of Grassy Lake, though you're never closer than 200 feet to it. The lake covers 38 acres. The trail soon curves east, briefly paralleling the Grassy Lake's north shore. When the trail swerves north, you've reached the turn-back point.

Nearby Trails

■ **Bear Lake Area County Forest trails** – A large number of trails crisscross this Barron County forest. Entering from the north side on Narrow Gauge Road, take the first gated trail on the left for a half-mile round trip to Lake 6.

■ **Kirby Lake Area County Forest** – On Fifth Street just before the road curves toward Kirby Lake, turn east onto a gated jeep trail. The path heads to Tamarack Lake; at the tee intersection, turn back for a 1.4-mile round trip.

■ **Maple Plain Area County Forest** – From 29-1/2 Avenue, take the gated jeep trail heading south. The trail crosses an unnamed creek flowing into Upper Waterman Lake. At the tee intersection, turn back for a half-mile round trip.

■ **Waterman Lake Area County Forest** – Off of County Road H south of 29th Avenue, take the gated jeep trail heading west. You'll walk past Lake 9-8A (It's more of a pond, really.) and end at scenic Black Duck Lake for a 2-mile round trip.

■ **Also see:** *Balsam Lake, Frederic/Luck, Rice Lake, Shell Lake/Sarona, Turtle Lake*

Danbury

Grouse Walk Trail
Big Bear Lake Nature Area

The Big Bear Lake Nature Trails offer three great day hiking opportunities for cabin-goers in the lake country of Burnett County.

All three trails are accessible from the same trailhead. The Grouse Walk Trail is the shortest at a half-mile.

To reach the trails, from Danbury take State Hwy. 77 north/east for a little more than 10 miles. Turn right/south onto Bear Lake Road; in about 1.5 miles, turn left/east into a sand parking lot. If you've reached the intersection with Lake 26 Road, you've missed the lot.

From the trailhead at the parking lot, go straight (the middle route). Going left takes you to the Big Bear Springs Trail for a 0.75 mile loop, which is fairly similar to the Grouse Walk Trail.

You're now heading clockwise on Grouse Walk Trail through a largely open grassland and shrubland with scattered pines, so you'll definitely need hat and sunscreen for the hike.

The nature trails are located in the rare Northwest Sands ecological landscape, which angles across this corner of Wisconsin from the St. Croix River to just short of the Lake Superior. Farm crops can't readily grow here because all that separates the surface from underlying bedrock is glacial drift – sand, gravel and silt left during the last ice age.

About midway through the Grouse Walk loop, an intersecting trail takes you east to the Big Bear Meadows Trail. The trail is more wooded and runs for 0.875 miles.

After curving southwest, the Grouse Walk Loop skirts the shoreline of a small pond that during dry years often is just a shallow depression. The loamy nature of the soil typically means that moisture drains fast through it.

Despite that, a number of kettle lakes from melted chunks of the last glacier exist across the region. Among them is nearby Big Bear Lake; though these nature trails are named for it, that lake actually is a good half-mile to the northeast.

Circling to Grouse Walk loop's south side, you'll head through a small grove. Pine, aspen, birch and oak dominate the few stands of trees in the Northwest Sands. Upon exiting the stand, you'll have returned to the parking lot.

Nearby Trails

■ **Danbury State Wildlife Area trails** – A goal post-shaped set of jeep trails form a square with County Road F, running through pine barrens and lowlands. Keep an eye out for snowshoe hare, ruffed grouse, beaver, mink and otter.

■ **Matthew Lourey State Trail** – Across the river in Minnesota, this trail runs for several miles roughly north to south through St. Croix State Park. A pleasant 2.3-mile segment heads from a trail center to Hay Creek.

■ **Namekagon Barrens Wildlife Area trails** – Take a walk down any of the gravel roads leading into these sand barrens for a hike into an Andy Griffith-like backwoods. Watch for sharp-tailed grouse and the upland sandpiper.

■ **Also see:** *Grantsburg, Minong, Siren, Spooner, Trego, Webster*

Drummond
Lake Owen Loop
North Country National Scenic Trail

Cabin-goers near Drummond can hike a segment of the 4,600-mile North Country National Scenic Trail in an enjoyable route I've christened the "Lake Owen Loop."

The North Country trail stretches from North Dakota to New York, cutting through four Wisconsin counties along the way. The Badger state boasts the highest percentage of completed and the longest continuous stretch of the trail in the country. In Bayfield County, the trail cuts through the popular Chequamegon National Forest.

About five miles long, the Lake Owen Loop is best done in autumn when the bug count is down and the trees ablaze with color. Early spring is good for avoiding mosquitos but may force you to cross two intermittent streams flush that time of year with snowmelt.

To reach the trail, from U.S. Hwy. 63 in Drummond, take North Lake Owen Drive, also known as Forest Road 213, south. You'll pass Roger Lake. When you come to Lake Owen, look for the intersection with Forest Road 216 (aka as Lake Owen Station Road). Stay on FR 213 and round the northern tip of Lake Owen. Turn right into the picnic grounds, where you'll park. A swimming beach also is on site.

Mixed hardwoods and pines

From the picnic area, look east and pick up the trail where it intersects the forest road. The North Country trail is fairly flat with elevation shifting about 50 feet during the hike.

Walk south, cutting between the northern tip of Lake Owen and a 35-foot deep pond. An intermittent stream connects it to the lake.

The trail follows the north shore of Lake Owen, forming a U. Mixed hardwoods and pines line the lake. Hemlock, oak, maple and white pine often stand high over the route.

As reaching the bottom of the U's western side, you'll cross a road. You're unlikely to see many people, though, as this side of Lake Owen is little used compared to its other shorelines, which sport camps and boat ramps.

At 1,323 acres with a maximum depth of 95 feet, Lake Owen boasts very clear water, making it an ideal habitat for largemouth and smallmouth bass, muskie, Northern pike, walleye and panfish.

Call of nesting loons

About midway at the U's bottom, there's a second intermittent stream to cross. You'll then spot Twin Lakes Campgrounds on the opposite short.

As coming up the U's eastern side, the trail veers away from lake. Watch for the wildlife that makes this area home. White-tailed deer, squirrels, chipmunks and frogs are certain to be seen, but also keep an eye out for other animals' tracks, especially those of raccoons. And keep your ears peeled for the call of loons, which nest on the area's lakes.

After crossing a forest road, you'll walk past a

pond to the right and then one to the left. Finally, you'll head past yet another pond, this one up to 14 feet deep, on the right.

Rejoining Forest Road 213, you can walk along-side it back to your vehicle. On the way you will first pass Forest Road 217, aka Cutacross Road, which goes north, and then Horseshoe Road, which goes south.

Upon reaching your start point, end the day with a picnic and swim.

Nearby Trails

■ **Anderson Grade Trail** – The 4-mile trail crosses the Rainbow Lake Wilderness Area from east to west over rolling terrain. Balsam fir, Northern hard-woods, paper birch and pines line the trail.

■ **Antler Trail** – Six trails make up the Drummond Ski Trail system southeast of town. This 2-mile route heads over gentle terrain through a Northern hardwood forest.

■ **Drummond Woods Trail** – Northeast of town in the Chequamegon National Forest, this 0.75-mile trail offers interpretive stops for those wishing to learn about the local woodlands. A segment of the North Country National Scenic Trail, it's a great route for seeing fall colors.

■ **North Country Scenic Trail segment in Porcu-pine Lake Wilderness** – Over a mix of rolling hills and fairly flat terrain, the trail cuts through a forest of hemlock, maple, oak and white pine. Expect to see white-tailed deer, loons and songbirds galore as well as signs of bear, coyote and fox.

■ **North Country Scenic Trail segment in Rainbow Lake Wilderness Area** – Six miles of the trail crosses the wilderness area from northwest to southwest. Built on an old narrow gauge logging bed, it passes four lakes.

■ **Two Lakes Campground Trail** – A 1.5-mile trail loops around Bass Lake near the campground in the national forest. Northern hardwoods and pines tower over the trail.

■ **Also see:** *Ashland, Cable, Clam Lake/Glidden, Iron River, Solon Springs*

Frederic/Luck

Ice Age National Scenic Trail segment Straight Lake Wilderness State Park

A naturalist's paradise, Straight Lake Wilderness State Park is Wisconsin's newest state park.

Formerly a Boy Scout camp, 2,800 acres of more than a dozen lakes and ponds may now only be accessed by foot, meaning no cars, pickup trucks, minivans, SUVs, ATVs, motorboats – not even bicycles or horses – are permitted.

While legions of Boy Scouts left lots of paths in the park, the Ice Age National Scenic Trail is the park's only designated trail. A three mile out-and-back segment running from the park's northwest parking lot to Rainbow Lake makes for an excellent and extremely peaceful walk.

To reach the trail, take State Hwy. 35 south from Frederic in Polk County. Turn left/east onto 280th Avenue. Just past 135th Street, 280th Avenue turns north, becoming 130th Street; at this turn is a parking lot.

The trailhead is at the road corner off of 280th Avenue. Head south into a mature Northern hardwoods forest. Some trees here are almost a century old.

After walking about 0.2 miles, the trail passes a 6.5 feet in diameter boulder. Known as a glacial erratic, it was brought here by the last glacier to cover the area some 10,000 years ago. Made of diorite, the rock came from north of Lake Superior.

About a 0.5 miles later, the trail begins to parallel the Straight River. Watch the waterway for a variety of animals that call the park their home; among them are black bears, fox, river otters and white-tailed deer on the ground and bald eagles, osprey, red-shouldered hawks, and the endangered trumpeter swan in the air. The forest also supports northern Wisconsin's largest population of cerulean warbler.

In another half mile, you'll arrive at Straight Lake's north shore. The lake formed after melting glacial water exploded through the ice, carving what is known as a tunnel channel. Today, bass, Northern pike and panfish call the waterbody home.

Close to 0.75 miles later, the end of the lake's north shore offers the best view of the tunnel channel you're hiking. Look up and down the river, and you'll notice you're in a long, narrow valley. This tunnel channel stretches 7.5 miles from where you began the hike at 280th Avenue southeast to Big Round Lake.

Continuing on, in short order you'll cross the Straight River and follow its south shore line. After a quarter mile, the trail comes to a widening in the river on the left and Rainbow Lake on the right/south. This marks a good spot to turn back.

Upon returning to the parking lot, if time and energy permit consider taking a brief excursion on the trail north of 280th Avenue. You'll be able to see the dark basalt of a 1.1-billion-year-old lava flow along the trail in about 0.2 miles. Plants do cover the ancient rock, but you should be able to spot it if keeping an eye out.

Nearby Trails

■ **Atlas County Park (unnamed trails)** – Short, unnamed trails amble through this park located between the Trade River and Long Trade Lake. The park includes picnic shelters perfect for that after-hike meal.

■ **Coon Lake Trail** – While some of the meandering paths making up this trail are steep, they offer great views of Coon Lake on Frederic's east side. The 41.7-acre man-made lake and the surrounding park is popular with local residents.

■ **Somers Lake Snowshoe Trail** – Three loops northwest of Frederic lead to scenic Somers Lake. The loops total five miles in length and head through a wooded area.

■ **Sterling Trail** – This 7-mile loop rambles across a classic Northwoods setting. Be forewarned that ATVs can use the trail June 1-Nov. 15.

■ **Also see:** *Balsam Lake, Grantsburg, Shell Lake/ Sarona, Siren, Webster*

Grantsburg
Sandrock Cliff Trail
St. Croix National Scenic Riverway

Unique, imposing bluffs set above a lush river await hikers of the Sandrock Cliffs Trail in Burnett County. Up to five miles of trails run through the area in the St. Croix National Scenic Riverway along the Minnesota border.

The southernmost trail – a 3-mile loop – offers more than enough scenery, but connecting trails allow cabin-goers with a little more energy to burn an additional two miles to hike.

To reach the Sandrock Cliffs Trail, take State Hwy. 70 toward the St. Croix River. A bridge on the highway connects the two states. Turn north into the Hwy. 70 Landing parking lots.

The trailhead sits on the parking lot's north side. Go clockwise on Loop A, which heads north along the river. Paths are fairly well maintained. There are some hills along the way, but they're nothing elementary school kids or older can't handle.

The first section of the loop follows a terrace along the river through a forest of red and white pines. Peace abounds as you walk across a soft and fragrant bed of pine needles.

River views also wow hikers on this trail. The St. Croix's clear, pristine water teems with smallmouth bass and freshwater mussels. This far north, the river channel also is fairly shallow, so thin sandy islands, riffles and shoals are prevalent.

Watch overhead for patrolling eagles and ospreys. They nest nearby.

On the ground, look for a variety of woodland animals, most notably porcupines, ducks and deer. Ash, maple, jack pine and aspen as well as an understory of ferns grow amid the dominant red and white pines.

About halfway through Loop A, turn onto Loop E, continuing the walk clockwise (or paralleling the river). Along this 0.3-mile loop, you'll spot the highlight of the trail: picturesque sandstone cliffs towering over a river side channel.

Stand on the sandstone cliffs, and you're atop what once was the bottom of a shallow sea from 500 million years ago. After the Cambrian-era sea evaporated, the sand deposits left behind were compressed into rock. Some 11,000 years ago during the end of the last ice age, raging flood waters carved out the riverway and exposed the sandstone.

The sandstone does give way easily, so remain clear of cliff edges. Also, carving or writing your name into the cliffs is illegal.

About half-way through Loop E, join Loop B for a 0.3-mile loop. Just a little bit onto Loop B are picnic tables perfect for lunch or a rest break with snack.

Bathrooms can be found about midway along Loop B. They're in the Tennessee Road parking lot.

Heading around the top curve of Loop B, its southern side rejoins Loop E, which in turn rejoins Loop A for a walk back to your parking lot near Hwy. 70.

As with any Northwoods trail, bring bug repellent to keep off deer ticks, and stay on the path so you don't walk into poison ivy.

This set of trails also can be accessed from its north side via Tennessee Road. Two additional trails – Loop C and Loop D, both 0.9 miles long – run north of Tennessee Road.

Dogs are allowed on all loops, so long as they remain leashed.

Nearby Trails

■ **Cedar Interpretive Trail** – This pleasant trail runs 1-mile round trip from the St. Croix River to Iron Creek in Governor Knowles State Forest. The boardwalk trail heads through a rare cedar grove.

■ **Fish Lake State Wildlife Area trail** – From

County Road O, a jeep trail makes a 3.2-mile loop past marshes. Eagles, sandhill cranes and trumpeter swans grace the wildlife area.

■ **Hay Creek Hiking Trail** – A 1.5-mile trail meanders through woodland at Crex Meadows Wildlife Area near Hay Creek. An observation platform at the trail's end allows hikers to spot a variety of waterfowl.

■ **Trade River Trails** – A series of loops, including a large one around a meadow, sit near the Trade River in neighboring Polk County. The wide trails head over easy, rolling terrain.

■ **Upper Phantom Cross Country Skiing & Hiking Trail** – A set of four loops offer a hike of up to 3.7 miles in length at Crex Meadows Wildlife Area. The wildlife area is part of one of the largest remaining pine barrens in the state.

■ **Willard Munger State Trail** – The Boundary Segment of this trail runs in Chengwatana State Forest, across the St. Croix River in Minnesota. Tamarack and burr oak dominate the forest, which boasts wild turkeys, beavers, mink and muskrat.

■ **Also see:** *Danbury, Frederic/Luck, St. Croix Falls, Siren, Webster*

Hayward
Black Lake Trail
Chequamegon National Forest

Hikers can learn about the history of Northwoods

logging while enjoying excellent water views on the Black Lake Trail in Ashland and Sawyer counties.

The Chequamegon National Forest sprawls across 858,400 acres in Ashland, Bayfield, Sawyer, Price, Taylor and Vilas counties. Most of Black Lake is in Ashland County – though to get there you'll spend most of your time driving through Sawyer County.

Any time from spring through autumn is a good time to hike Black Lake, but be sure to bring mosquito and bug spray if going in summer.

Original forest logged off

To reach Black Lake, from Hayward take County Road B east for about 23 miles. Turn left/north onto Barker Lake Road (County Road W goes right/south). Upon entering the national forest, Barker Lake Road becomes Forest Road 174. You will need a permit to park your vehicle in the national forest, but there's no entry fee.

After about 10 miles, turn right onto Forest Road 172, also known as Black Lake Road. Just past Mud Lake, turn left/north onto Forest Road 173, aka North Black Lake Road. You'll soon come to the south end of Black Lake; once there, turn right/east onto Forest Road 1668. Park at the campground, which is at the lake's midpoint on its eastern shore.

To find the trailhead, look west in the parking lot for the trail sign. Follow the four-mile loop clockwise (go left/south) so that the trail's nine interprettive signs appear in order. You may want to pick up a brochure that explains the area's logging history.

White pine grew around the lake when loggers arrived in the 1880s. During the next 30 years, they cleared the region of it, floating the logs down Fishtrap Creek and the Chippewa River to sawmills in Chippewa Falls. From there, it was rafted to the Mississippi River all the way to St. Louis. During the 1910s to mid-1920s, hemlock and Northern hardwoods were logged.

Today, primarily birch, red pine, and spruce trees surround the 129-acre lake, which always appears clear and placid.

Thank a glacier for the brilliant blue waters. The lake sits where enormous blocks of melting ice were left when the glacier retreated at the end of the last ice age. Today, the lake hosts largemouth bass, northern and muskie pike, and walleye. Elk, white-tailed deer and loons inhabit the shorelines.

At the campground, hikers can find water at hand pumps, toilets, and a grassy swimming beach. Dogs and other pets are allowed on the trail but must be on a leash at all times.

Blue and Orange trails
Town of Hayward Recreational Forest

Among the Northwoods' newest hiking trails can be found at the Town of Hayward Recreational Forest in Sawyer County. The 160-acre facility opened in spring 2011 and is quickly becoming a popular cross country skiing and snowshoeing destination. In spring, summer and fall, it's also a great place for day hiking.

Indeed, combining the rec forest's Blue and Orange trails into a 1.6-mile walk takes you through a woods past a wetland and then a scenic lake where wildlife is abundant.

Dry periods probably are the best time to visit the forest, as deer ticks can be a problem in the wet grass that makes up the trail surface; when the grass is mowed, though, this isn't an issue. In addition, the forest is closed to hiking during Wisconsin's annual gun deer hunting season, which runs the Saturday before to the Sunday after Thanksgiving.

To reach the rec forest, from U.S. Hwy. 63 at Hayward's south end, take Vermont Street north. The street curves west, becoming Johnson Street and upon leaving the Hayward city limits turns into County Hill Road. Drive for about two miles. Past North Gomey Road, the entrance to the park will be on your left, just beyond the gravel pit. The entry road takes you to the parking lot.

Wooded land

From there, hikers have the choice of two trails, which in turn lead to several loops. Take the one on the lot's south side and to the right; it's nicknamed the Blue Trail because of its color on the rec forest map.

The Blue Trail's first segment runs straight and leads to a loop. When you come to the tee intersection, you've reached that loop.

At that junction, go right. Another straight section runs for a third of a mile. You'll pass through an oak, aspen and pine forest. The terrain is rolling to hilly.

When coming to the next trail junction, go right onto the Orange Trail, a short 0.49-mile loop. You'll pass a wetlands and then curve away from it.

On the next sharp curve, you'll come to the Konieczny Lake shore. It's named for the property owner from who the land for the rec forest was purchased in 2007.

At the next trail junction, you'll rejoin the Blue Trail. Go right. The path continues briefly alongside the lake, then the trail and shoreline veer away from another.

More amenities coming

You'll pass three more junctions as you round back toward your starting point. These are connecting trails that run through the forest's southeast corner.

At the fourth junction, you've reached the segment of the Blue Trail that you came in on before coming to the very first loop. Take this segment by going right, and head back to parking lot.

While the forest is underdeveloped compared to the typical state or county park – there are no bathrooms or water – this does make for a stronger back-to-nature experience. In any case, plans are underway to improve amenities; in fact, a warming house was recently added.

One other benefit: Pets are allowed at the rec forest.

Namekagon-Laccourt Oreilles Portage Trail
St. Croix National Scenic Riverway

Though the Namekagon-Laccourt Oreilles Portage Trail memorializes a famous 18th century route where fur traders and explorers carried their canoes between rivers, hikers will head through a landscape much changed from that day. In fact, those fur traders and explorers probably wouldn't recognize the wild area.

Located near Hayward in the St. Croix National Scenic Riverway, the modern trail is very close to the original portage route. A fur trader even operated a winter post during 1784 near the trail. That portage route sprung up because travelers hoping to avoid problems with Sioux Indians near the St. Croix and Mississippi rivers junction decided to instead reach the continent's greatest waterway by making a series of portages from the Namekagon to the Chippewa River, which joins the Mississippi at Lake Pepin downstream from the Sioux.

To reach the portage trail from Hayward, go south on State Hwy. 27. A historic marker erected in 1955 commemorates the portage. Turn left/west onto Rainbow Road then right/north onto Rolf Road. Upon entering the scenic riverway, take the first left/west. A parking lot will be on the right, and the trailhead begins there.

An easy, 0.8-mile loop, hikers will head through a second growth forest of mixed hardwoods and pines.

Those using the portage trail in the 1700s found quite different flora growing there. At the time, this flat sandy area largely consisted of red and jack pines with white pines on the surrounding higher grounds. Most of that was logged off during the late 1800s, however, and the result is an area now dominated by maples, oaks, birch, red pine and spruce.

Logging and later small dams collaborated to change life in the Namekagon by leaving the shoreline open to sunlight. The result was an increase in the water temperature, which decimated some fish populations common during fur trading times.

At the loop's westernmost edge, hikers can take a short spur trail to the Namekagon, and it's well worth the walk, for the blue river is scenic. One thing the 101-mile long tributary to the St. Croix River does retain is its Ojibwa name, which means "at the place abundant with sturgeons."

Today, bass, blacknose dace, brook trout, brown trout, cheek chub, Johnny Darter, mudminnow, northern pike, sculpin and sucker primarily live in the river. Rainbow Creek, which runs south of the trail and feeds the Namekagon, is a rainbow trout fishery.

Along the trail, hikers also can cross wetlands over a boardwalk. Watch and listen for bull frogs, turtles and waterfowl common in the area.

Nearby Trails

■ **Short Swing Trail** – A few miles east of town, the Flambeau River State Forest offers a number of hiking trails. Among the easiest is the 1.1-mile Short Swing Trail, a loop that is easily found from an access trail in the parking lot of County Road W.

■ **West Torch Trail short loop** – Northeast of town, a trio of stacked loops form the West Torch Trail in the Chequamegon National Forest. From the parking lot, take the first (and shortest) of the loops for a roughly 2-mile hike through a wooded area.

■ **Also see:** *Cable, Clam Lake/Glidden, Minong, Spooner, Trego*

Hudson

Burkhardt Trail
Willow River State Park

A walk alongside a scenic river gorge, a waterfall, and some impressive overlooks await hikers on the Burkhardt Trail in Willow River State Park near Hudson.

The trail actually is three miles of connecting paths. It's also known as the Pink Path because of its color on state park maps.

To reach Willow River State Park, take Exit 4 from Interstate 94, heading north on U.S. Hwy. 12 for about 1.6 miles. Take County Road U for about 0.3 miles to County Road A, where you'll continue for another 1.5 miles. Pass the park's entrance on the road's left side and turn left onto County Road I. Take a left onto River Road (aka 115th Avenue) and then make a quick left into the River Road parking lot (You'll need to pay an entrance fee or sport an annual state park pass.). The trailhead is on the parking lot's south side.

The path begins by heading southwest along the Willow River bottoms. The marsh-like region boasts tall grasses and during summer a number of wildflowers. Watch for white-tailed deer in the brush, eagles soaring overhead, and during summer butterflies and dragonflies flitting about you. Frogs and variety of birds also are abundant along the riverfront.

Upon coming to the first fork, go left, into a wooded area and then into a large meadow. Aspen, oak, maple and of course willow trees abound. At the next fork, again go left. You'll head onto a bluff to an impressive overlook of the waterway and the gorge it has cut.

The trail then heads downward. At the next fork, veer left for the multi-level Willow River Falls. The rock on the gorge walls' lowest levels is about 600 million years old.

You can take a stairwell about 100-feet down to the falls. Sometimes you'll catch people wading through the falls; this is not advised for small children.

You can treat the trail to the falls as a spur and simply head back the way you came, or you can continue onward. If choosing the latter, cross the wood footbridge over the river but then turn back or you'll find yourself on another trail on the wrong side of the waterway.

Upon turning back, the trail meanders northward, ultimately forming a loop.

At the next trail intersection, go left. You'll then be heading back to the parking lot. At the next fork, turn left again, and you'll find yourself on the trail winding along the river bottoms, which is where you started.

Depending on whether or not you turned around at the falls, the hike ranges from 2 to 4 miles in length. The park is open every day of the year from 6 a.m. to 11 p.m.

Nearby Trails

■ **Kinnickinnic County Forest trails** – A series of unnamed trails run across 80 acres of pines planted by grade school children during the 1960s. Most of the trails run north-south.

■ **Purple Trail** – Traveling south to Kinnickinnic State Park near Prescott, this 1-mile trail offers great views of the delta where the park's namesake flows into the blue St. Croix River. You'll pass through an old-growth oak forest on the way.

■ **Siem Trail** – Located in the Homestead Parklands on Perch Lake, the 1-mile trail starts at a beach and runs along the western side of a kettle – a lake formed several thousand years ago when a retreating glacier left a chunk of ice that depressed the land with the meltwater filling the hole.

■ **Trout Brook Trail** – Another impressive trail at Willow River State Park is this 1.4-mile loop that takes hikers through red pine stands and open prairie. You'll be able to spot great blue heron, ducks and snapping turtles.

■ **Also see:** *Osceola, Somerset*

Iron River

Iron River National Fish Hatchery trails
Iron River National Fish Hatchery

This day hiking trail north of Iron River offers the opportunity to learn about the life cycle of fish and the importance of national fish hatcheries.

Three miles of trails cut through 1,200 acres of the U.S. Fish and Wildlife Service's Iron River National Fish Hatchery facility. A 2.4-mile segment of those interpretive trails with a stop at the visitor center can make for a fun and educational day.

To reach the hatchery, take County Road A north from Iron River for 6.6 miles. Turn left/east on Fairview Road. The hatchery entrance is in one mile.

Park at the visitor center. Before hitting the trail, check in at the center.

For the trailhead, continue walking south on the road you drove in on. After about 0.2 miles, turn right onto a jeep trail heading southeast. The trail enters a wooded area.

The fish hatchery's location should come as no surprise. It's only a few miles from Lake Superior, as evidenced by the pine barrens on the Bayfield Peninsula that that trail passes through.

In 0.3 miles, take the trail south. After another 0.2 miles, the trail curves west.

The hatchery annually rears about 2 million trout that are then placed in Lake Superior, Lake Michigan, Lake Huron and some of their tributaries. Research also is conducted here. It was established in 1979.

About 0.5 miles later, the trail reaches Weidenaar Road. To avoid walking alongside the highway, turn back here.

Upon returning to the parking lot, be sure to stop at the visitor center. Aquariums in the hatchery's Main Building and the early rearing tankroom also will be interesting to see, especially for children.

When at the hatchery, remind children with you to keep their hands out of the raceways. Doing so helps prevent disease from spreading among fish.

Nearby Trails

■ **Ahmeek Lake Walking Trail** – Southeast of town off Luke Hughes/Pero Road, a 4.4-mile trail runs to County Road A past ponds through a new growth forest. The route is part of the North Country National Scenic Trail.

■ **Flag River Walking Trail** – North of town on Flag Road a half-mile from Battle Axe Road, the trail meanders west near the Flag River. Groves of Northern hardwoods and evergreens shade the path.

■ **Long Lake Picnic Area Trail** – This 1.2-mile trail in the Chequamegon National Forest circles Long Lake and includes a boardwalk into a marsh. A picnic area is on the grounds; a parking fee is required.

■ **North Country National Scenic Trail segment** – West of town, a segment of this multi-state trails runs through the Brule River State Forest. From the parking lot off of State Hwy. 27 near Radio Station Road, take the trail north for about two miles to Rush River Road; turn left onto Rush Road River, crossing Hwy. 27, for views of Big Lake.

■ **Ruth Lake walking trails** – On Ruth Lake Road, a half mile from the County Road A intersection, trails begin on both sides of the highway. Go west to skirt the wooded southern end of Lake Ruth in the Chequamegon National Forest.

■ **Tomahawk Lake trails** – On Moore Road about 1.5 miles from the Island Lake Road intersection, walking paths run through wooded areas. Trails begin on either side of the road.

■ **Tri-County Corridor Trail segment** – The trail connecting Superior and Ashland runs through Iron River. East of town, take the segment from Topside Road east past Wentzel Lake and a pond to Forest Road 417 for a 3.8-mile one-way hike.

■ **Also see:** *Ashland, Drummond, Poplar/Brule, Solon Springs, Washburn*

Mellen
Doughboys' Nature Trail
Copper Falls State Park

Hikers can tour Wisconsin's geological history in some of the most breathtaking scenery this side of the Mississippi on Doughboys' Nature Trail at Copper Falls State Park. Located in Ashland County, the trail follows the Bad River and Tyler Forks past Copper and Brownstone waterfalls and a series of cascades.

Summer and early fall mark the best time to hike the trail. A portion of it closes during the winter as ice leaves rock stairs slippery and unsafe.

To reach Copper Falls State Park, from Mellen take State Hwy. 169 north. Upon passing Loon

Lake, enter the park by turning left onto Copper Falls Road. A vehicle admission sticker or state trail pass – which costs as low as $3 for Wisconsin visitors making a daily visit to $35 for out-of-state visitors seeking an annual pass – is required for entry.

The road leads to a parking lot near the pet area. From there, head northwest to the picnic area. Doughboys' Nature Trail starts near the concession building. The thick red clays you'll spot near that building weren't there a few thousand years ago. At the time, Lake Superior – made larger than it is today by melting glaciers – covered the park. The clay and granite boulders were left here by those ice sheets after dragging them down from Canada.

Billion-year-old lava rock

Doughboys' Nature Trail actually consists of several sections of other trails that form a nice 1.7-mile loop at the park's heart. Begin the trail by taking a footbridge over the Bad River. Once across the bridge, you'll notice an observation tower is to the left. Go right for the view of Copper Falls.

The 29-foot waterfall is the first of many drops the Bad River takes in the park. The river for the past 200 million years slowly has slowly carved out the canyon through this 1 billion-year-old lava rock left by ancient volcanoes.

At Bad and Tyler Forks rivers junction, you'll

spot Brownstone Falls. The two rivers join spectacularly with Tyler Forks plunging over a hard red lava edge into the rugged gorge. The black walls rise between 60-100 feet above the swirling water.

White cedar trees line the gorge. A plethora of other hardwoods – aspen, basswood, hemlock, ironwood, paper birch, red oak, red pine, sugar maple, white pine, and yellow birch – cover the park, making for impressive autumn walks.

The trail then veers left, following Bad River as it flows on hard, erosion-resistant red lava. When this basalt was formed, the North American continent literally was splitting in half, resulting in a rift full of volcanoes. Lake Superior in part exists because its basin consists of this lava.

Canyon walls tipped on their sides

This geology changes slightly as the trail passes Devil's Gate, in which the river flows over conglomerate rocks left by ancient streams. The canyon walls showing these different layers of sediment sit almost on their sides as the ground settled and hard lavas shifted upward.

At the footbridge, go right and cross the Bad River. The trail follows the waterway on the opposite shoreline, offering different perspective of Devil's Gate. It then briefly joins the North Country National Scenic Trail; stay to right and keep following the river. Within a few minutes of walking, the trail passes the river fork again, offering hikers a different view of Brownstone Falls.

By this point in the trail, you've probably noticed a great amount of wildlife. While the trail usually is too busy for the park's larger denizens – white-tailed deer, elk, black bears and gray wolves – to come close, chipmunks and red and gray squirrels as well a number of songbirds are abundant. You'll also likely spot the big northern raven, great pile-ated woodpecker, and chickadees. Visitors in June and July likely will see banded purple and tiger swallowtail butterflies.

If lucky, you also may sight ruffed grouse, eag-les, turkey vultures, raccoons, fishers, skunks, por-cupines (well, maybe not so lucky with skunks). Wood turtles and wood frogs also live near the shores, as do five different types of snakes, none of which are poisonous.

Final leg of the trail

The trail briefly follows Tyler Forks River past the Cascades, which is supported by black lava. A footbridge takes hikers across the Tyler Forks, which was named for John Tyler, a ship captain who surveyed the area for the Indian Agency.

You'll then head back on the opposite shore of Tyler Forks River past the Cascades and Brown-stone Falls. Upon passing the river junction, head south along the Bad River shore back to the picnic area/concession stand where you began.

Miscellaneous notes: Pets are not allowed on the

trail. The first half mile is accessible for people with disabilities.

Penokee Mountain Trail
Chequamegon National Forest

Cabin-goers to northern Wisconsin can hike across the remnants of an ancient mountain range that once soared as high as the Alps.

The Penokee Mountain Trail – a cross country ski trail in winter, a day hiking trail in summer – also is part of the North Country National Scenic Trail. It actually consists of three loops, which depending on your time and energy levels, can be done separately for as short as a two-mile hike to one up to 5.3 miles.

Autumn makes for a lovely time to hike the trail, as the rugged uplands offer superb views of the multi-colored trees in the valley below.

To reach the trail, from Mellen drive about 3.5 miles on County Road GG. Turn right into a parking lot. A fee is required to park. The trailhead sits at the parking lot's north end. Follow the trail counterclockwise.

Range once as tall as the Alps

As you're in the Chequamegon National Forest, walking paths are in good shape, but you will be going up and down some hills if you take the longest route.

The first loop runs for two miles along the area's

eastern side. You'll head through a hemlock forest that provides a home to white-tailed deer, bears and ruffed grouse.

Reaching the north side, you'll get a spectacular view of the valley below, which maples, oaks and basswood with an understory of balsam fir and white pine dominate. You actually are walking along one of the highest ridges in Wisconsin; the surface of Lake Superior, which sits 19 miles to the north, is 850 feet below your elevation.

The ridge with its granite ledges are all that remain of an ancient mountain range that once towered more than 10,000 feet high. Rock folds suggest what this range must have looked like some 500-600 million years ago: lofty peaks and deep valleys, similar to the Alps. These mountains are among some of the oldest in the world, predating animal life on land.

What remains 200 million years later...

For the past 200 million years, the mountains have been slowly eroding into a low, slightly undulating flat area called a peneplain. The Penokee Range, which stretches about 80 miles long and is up to a mile wide, is known as a monadnock because its resistant rocks leave them standing above this plain.

The three trail loops upon this monadnock are fairly easy to follow, as several signs indicate the North Country Trail's route. In addition, ski maps of the trail can be downloaded or picked up at area establishments.

Should you be up for a longer walk, staying to the right rather than looping back by going left at trail junctions, will allow you to extend the walk to 3.2 miles on the ridge's northern side. That loop in turn can be extended to 5.3 miles, which covers the trail's western portion. If opting for this longer route, you will twice cross a quarry road. The approaches at these roads are abrupt declines. You'll also come across an Adirondack shelter, a great place for taking a rest break.

Nearby Trails
■ **Juniper Rock Overlook segment** – West of town, pick up the North Country National Scenic Trail off of Forest Road 202. Walk east for a little more than a half-mile to the overlook of the Marengo River. You can extend the hike for another mile to old Swedish settlements and additional overlooks.

■ **Red Granite Trail** – The 2.5-mile round trip trail runs to Red Granite Falls in the southern portion of Copper Falls State Park. Dogs are welcomed on the walking path.

■ **Takesson Trail loops** – An inner loop runs for 1.6 miles and an outer loop for 2.5 miles, offering picturesque views of the Bad River in Copper Falls State Park. Both loops ramble through a mature hardwood forest, but the outer loop is hillier.

■ **Also see:** *Ashland, Cable, Clam Lake/Glidden, Drummond*

Minong
Totagatic Trail Loop A

Multiple ski loop trails in winter serve as great day hiking paths in summer for cabin-goers in the Minong area.

Of the four Totagatic Ski Trail loops, try Loop A. At two miles round trip, it's the shortest as well as the closest to the parking lot so is easy to locate.

To reach the trail system, head a little more than a mile north of Minong village on U.S. Hwy. 53. At the second, or northernmost, intersection with Lakeside Road, turn left/east into the parking lot.

A jeep trail runs west from the parking lot for 0.25 miles. Most of the trail is mixed hardwoods, consisting of sugar and red maple and basswood. On other loops, trails head through groves of re-planted trees.

At the first divide in trail, head straight (or left/west) to do the route clockwise. You're now officially on Loop A.

The trails run through a border area between two ecosystems – the North Central Forest and the Northwest Sands regions. The major difference is the former's soil is only 5-10 feet above the bedrock while the latter can have a separation of several hundred feet. In part because of this, the North

Central Forest is better able to hold hardwood trees such as maples whereas the Northwest Sands is pine and shrubland.

In 0.25 miles, the trail comes to a junction. Go right/north on a section of trail shared with Loop B.

The North Central Forest also covers a lot of territory in Wisconsin; it can be found in 19 counties and stretches into Michigan's Upper Peninsula. Often when thinking of the "Northwoods," an image of the North Central Forest is what comes to mind for most Wisconsinites and travelers to the state.

The next trail junction comes in about 0.1 miles; at it, go right/north. The trail you didn't take heads onto Loop B, which in turn connects with loops C and D.

"Totagatic" is derived from the Ojibwa word "Totogan," which means "boggy river." The trails, however, don't go near their namesake river, which is to the north by a few miles. In any case, the Native Americans' name for the area that includes Minong village and these ski trails translates to "Pleasant Valley."

After about 0.25 miles, Loop A veers east and gradually curves south. In little more than 0.9 miles, you'll reach the access trail that leads to the parking lot; go left/east back to the lot.

Nearby Trails
■ **Brule River State Forest Annex trails** – North of

town in Douglas County along County Road G lies a small area of planted forests along the Eau Claire River with multiple jeep trails running through them. From the end of the county road, hike west until the road curves north; take each of the three spur trails to the river for a 1.7-mile walk.

■ **Wild Rivers State Trail segment** – The former rail line turned hiking trail heads through town on the way from Trego to Gordon. Starting at South Limits Road, head south on the trail to Lakeside Lake for a roughly four-mile round trip.

■ **Also see:** *Cable, Danbury, Hayward, Solon Springs, Trego*

Osceola
Ridgeview Trail
Osceola Bedrock Glades S.N.A.

Travelers to Wisconsin can hike across billion-year-old lava flows while seeing a rare, unique glade ecosystem when taking the Ridgeview Trail at the Osceola Bedrock Glades State Natural Area.

Located north of Osceola, from State Hwy. 35 turn north on County Road S. After passing 93rd Avenue and crossing two creeks (a total of 1.1 miles), turn left (or west) onto the next unpaved road and park there. The trailhead is to the southeast along the roadside.

The trail leads south into the natural area. You can take two loops, one short (0.9-mile loop) and the other long (about 1.5 miles loop; if taking the up-hill route, 2.1 miles loop). You may have to go cross-country a little, but the vegetation generally is low and easy to walk across.

Begin by heading a tenth of a mile roughly southwest toward a hill. The greenery of the thin-trunked trees forms a marked contrast with the black rock jutting out of the hard ground. For 200 million years, lava flowed across the region, which at the time was a rift zone where the land to the west and that to the east shifted apart from one another.

At the hill's base, turn right and walk about a third of a mile. Because of the hard, flat volcanic bedrock beneath your feet, very few plants can grow here. Most common are ferns, mosses, low-growing herbs and fungi.

The area itself is rare. In fact, only three other bedrock glade ecosystems exist in Wisconsin.

To take the short trail, upon reaching the hill's corner head up to its top for 0.3 miles. The hill summit with its outcropping is about half of this distance. The summit with its basalt outcroppings feels more like a West Coast mountain top than a Midwestern hill. At the hill's base, upon coming to County Road S, go north 0.2 miles back to your vehicle.

For the longer trail, instead of turning at the hill's corner go 0.1 miles northwest to a rock outcropping. The black, moss-covered rocks gives the area an otherworldly feel. Walk around it, and enjoy your bluff-top view overlooking the St. Croix River; you're at about 876 feet elevation. If children are with you, make sure they stay back from the bluff's edge.

The trail passes through oak woodland and in areas where the volcanic rock is close to the surface, the bedrock glade. The rare prairie flame flower can be spotted here. In September, the white arrow-leaved aster blooms, which makes for an interesting accent color before tree leaves have changed to their fall colors.

Despite the harsh environment for plants, a number of animals live in the bedrock glade. With the thin trees, owls are easy to spot. Around Labor Day, some interesting insects come out. The giant swallowtail caterpillar, which looks more like a knotty branch than a furry little creature, can be seen crawling on prickly ash, and you'll likely sight a lyre-tipped spreadwing perching on a twig-like branch. During the summer, mosquitoes can be ubiquitous, so don't forget the bug repellent.

The trail loops 0.7 miles around the back of the hill. At about 0.2 miles on this loop, you will join a jeep trail, which you can follow for more ease of walking.

On the southeast side of hill's base, when the trail reaches County Road S, head north for a little more than 0.2 miles back to your vehicle.

Alternately, you can follow a trail west up to the

hill summit and then upon coming down it on its west side, rejoin the trail where you began your loop, retracing it back to your vehicle.

Ridge View (Osceola/Chisago) Trails
St. Croix National Scenic Riverway

Fantastic river views beneath a lush forest canopy await visitors to the Ridge View Trails near Osceola.

Not to be confused with Ridgeview Trail at the adjacent Osceola Bedrock Glades State Natural Area, this pair of trails actually are two loops that only locals really know about. They run through the St. Croix National Scenic Riverway and the Osceola State Fish Hatchery on a bluff overlooking the St. Croix River's back channel.

To reach the two loops, take State Hwy. 35 north of Osceola and turn north onto County Road S. The two trailheads are on the road's west (or driver's) side. Both trailheads have their own parking areas off of the road. Just beyond 93rd Avenue is the southern-most parking area, which actually is an excellent trailhead for either loop.

From that trailhead, head west. At the first fork, continue straight to hike the Chisago Loop. Slightly more than one mile long, it's the northern trail. Alternatively, at the fork you can head left, or south, for the Osceola Loop, which is about twice as long as its counterpart. Either trail ranges from easy to moderate in difficulty, so the distance you can handle, especially if you have children along, really determines which one to take.

If heading onto the Chisago Loop, you'll be hiking clockwise around the trail. It's mostly level and sometimes covered in a bed of pine needles or ancient, billion-year-old trap rock. You'll see a number of these basalt outcroppings along the way. Some neat dead end spurs off the trail offer great views of the river below.

About two-thirds of way around, be careful of taking a fork to the right/north, lest you end up at the second of the road's two parking lots (and is the one where you didn't park your vehicle).

If opting for the Osceola Loop, upon reaching the main trail, go left/south, so you take it clockwise. This saves the best views for the last half of the hike.

You'll begin by heading through a pine and deciduous forest in which the canopy arches over the trail. About half-way through as you turn north, between the trees you can see river's back channel and hear the rush of a rapids-filled stream in the canyon below the bluffs. Watch for pits off of the trail; they are believed to have been made many decades ago by Native Americans.

Either trail is excellent for viewing birds – scarlet tanagers, eagles, turkeys, grouse – and other forest-loving wildlife. Forest plants you're likely to spot include marsh marigolds and large maple trees.

Nearby Trails

■ **Lake O' the Dalles Nature Trail** – To the north at Wisconsin Interstate State Park, a one-mile loop circles the 23-acre Lake O' the Dalles. The trail offers exceptional opportunities to view wildlife.

■ **Riverside Trail** – Cross the border into Minnesota for William O'Brien State Park, where this 1.5-mile trail will take you to the shores of Alice Lake and the St. Croix River. There are benches every 900 feet.

■ **Stower Seven Lakes Trail** – This trail cuts across Polk County beginning (or ending, depending on your perspective) east of town at Lotus Lake. You can walk about two miles along Horse Creek to Horse Lake for a 4-mile round trip.

■ **Also see:** *Amery, Hudson, St. Croix Falls, Somerset*

Poplar/Brule

Amnicon Falls island trails
Amnicon Falls State Park

Hikers can view the results of an earthquake from 500 million years ago while walking the island trails at Amnicon Falls State Park.

Known as the Douglas Fault, this split in the earth stretches from Ashland to near the Twin Cities. Much of the bedrock sits at 50-60 degree angles, offering sights reminiscent of those along California's San Andreas Fault. All of these millennia later, the fault line still effects the course of rivers – which is to hikers' visual advantage.

To reach the state park, from U.S. Hwy. 2 go west of Poplar. Turn left, or north, onto County Road U. The park entry is in 0.3 miles. A vehicle admission sticker is required to enter.

Continue past the contact station across the bridge over the river and park in the first lot to the right; if it's full, continue on, taking the first road to right for another parking lot. Presuming you got a parking space in the first lot, pick up the trail at the picnic shelter and go right toward the Amnicon River. Listen for the sound of gurgling water, present the moment you open your vehicle's doors.

Because of the river's high mineral content, the waterway sometimes can appear the color of root beer; it's clean, though, and swimming is allowed in designated areas. The river ultimately meanders north, flowing into Lake Superior.

River island

The trail follows the Amnicon for about a quarter mile past another parking area and shelter (if you parked in the second lot, this is where you pick up the trail). Cross the river over a footbridge, which deposits you on an island where the waterway splits into two channels.

Go left for a view of Snake Pit Falls. While not particularly wide, the falls is 25 feet high with the water channeled between two stone works.

Continuing on, the trail loops around the island, offering a view of where the river divides. You also can garner a view of Lower Amnicon Falls. It tumbles over sandstone laid here more than 400 million years ago when streams flowed into a warm tropical ocean that covered Wisconsin.

The trail from there crosses the river via the 55-foot long Horton covered bridge, one of the park's major attractions. Originally a highway bridge at another spot on the Amnicon, it was moved here in 1930. It is one of only five Horton bridges that still exist. Besides experiencing history, hikers crossing the bridge are afforded two picturesque views as well – you can see waterfalls from both sides.

Lower and Upper Amnicon falls

After crossing the bridge off the island, go left for a different view of Lower Amnicon Falls. Erosion has smoothed out the sandstone cliff here.

You might be pleasantly surprised by the amount of wildlife at the park. Black bear, coyote, fox, porcupine, raccoon, squirrels and white-tailed deer abound. Beaver, mink and otter – or at least their tracks – often can be spotted along the shore. A number of birds, including ruffed grouse and songbirds, also can be seen.

Backtrack and at the bridge continue straight, walking along the river banks for a view of Upper Amnicon Falls. The river rumbles over dark basalt, or solidified lava that formed here a billion years ago.

Canadian boulders and glacial potholes

If you've noticed a number of gray, sparkling boulders, that's non-native rock. Though the rock is tens of millions of years old, glaciers brought this granite gneiss here from Canada during the last ice age. Potholes in the rock also are fairly recent; swift-moving waters from melting glaciers drilled them out only a few thousand years ago.

Return to the bridge and cross back to the island. Go left for an island view of Upper Amnicon Falls.

Finally, cross the first bridge you took to reach the island. Follow along the same the path that you originally took to the island, maybe pausing for a picnic or snack. Past the second water source, the trail splits; go right to get back to your vehicle.

Nearby Trails

■ **Bayfield Road Trail** – The 2.25-mile loop trail in the Brule River State Forest passes through red oak stands that recently came under attack by two-lined chestnut borer, offering insights into the woodlands and a tree species man is trying to rescue. A connecting trail leads to the Copper Range Campground.

■ **North Country National Scenic Trail** – The scenic trail runs roughly north-south through the lower half of the Brule River State Forest. A peaceful segment to walk is from State Hwy. 27 (north of Radio Station Road) south to County Road S for a 6-mile round trip.

■ **Stoney Hill Nature Trail** – The 1.7-mile loop offers fantastic views of the Brule River Valley. Sections can be steep, but there is a rest stop and overlook at the hill's top.

■ **Tri-County Corridor Trail** – Connecting Superior to Ashland, the trail heads through Poplar. To get away from the highway noise, try the roughly 2.25-mile one-way segment between Midway Road and County Road F.

■ **Also see:** *Iron River, Solon Springs, Superior*

Rice Lake
Wild Rivers Trail

A walk through pleasant wooded areas and scenic farmland await users of the Wild Rivers Trail near Rice Lake. The trail runs for around 100 miles across three counties on an old Omaha and Soo Line Railroad rail line connecting the city to Superior.

A good place to experience the trail is at its southern end. Park north of the Rice Lake city limits at the Tuscobia Trail junction on County Road SS, near its intersection with U.S. Hwy. 53. You can head south for about four miles into Rice Lake at West Knapp Street. Arrange to have someone bring you back to where you parked, or turn around at any time on the trail.

The parking lot sits east of County Road SS, and you'll need to take the Tuscobia Trail west across the highway to reach the Wild Rivers Trail. Turn left or south onto the Wild Rivers Trail, which parallels County Road SS into Rice Lake. Turn right, and the trail heads to Haugen, Spooner, Trego, Minong, Gordon, Solon Springs and ends in Superior.

In addition to plenty of parking and its proximity to a major town for an enjoyable meal or shopping afterward, the trail section heading south is an excellent shape with compacted gravel making up the surface.

The first half mile or so heads through a typical deciduous forest that Wisconsin is famous for. In autumn, the trail's varied trees alight in an array of red, yellow and orange leaves. Upon crossing County Road BB, however, the woods gives way to pretty farm fields that look best when green in August.

A little more than two miles later, you can glimpse through the deepening treeline a tributary that ultimately flows into nearby Stump Lake. As the region becomes more wooded, you'll actually cross the serpentine waterway over a quaint bridge.

Expect to spot white-tailed deer, rabbits, squirrels and chipmunks – and if lucky, fox – along the way. Songbirds are plentiful, and hawks soar overhead.

On weekends, anticipate a variety of other users. Mountain bikers, horseback riders and ATVers also frequent the trail. In winter, you'll share the route with snowmobilers, cross country skiers and snowshoers.

The trail grows increasingly urban as reaching 22-1/2 Street with a good end spot at Knapp Street, where your designated waiter can park the vehicle. Pit toilets are available at the trailhead.

Nearby Trails

■ **Cedar Lake Area County Forest trails** – As with all Barron County Forests, several unnamed trails crisscross the wooded area. Try the northernmost one, off of Valley Road, which heads west for 2.5 miles through a nice mix of hardwoods; it ends at a gate just shy of Red Cedar Lake.

■ **Cedar Lake Sections 5 & 6 County Forest trails** – Off of North Townline Road just east of 24th Street, a trail runs roughly north-south for about 1.5 miles before coming to a tee intersection. You'll walk through a thick hardwood forest.

■ **Cedar Side Walking Trail** – If you need to make a trip into town, consider this beautiful trail that runs alongside the Red Cedar River. Plenty wide and some of it paved, you can take different-length segments based on your abilities.

■ **Mikana Area County Forest** – On Swamp Road

upon coming to Mirror Lake, take the gated trail going north. You'll skirt the shorelines of the lake and then Lake 20-10. Turn around at the gate where the trail splits for about a 1-mile round trip.

■ **Moon Lake Biking and Walking Trail** – Located at the site of a former municipal airport, this 1.5-mile round trip trail heads to and along scenic Moon Lake. The trail is wide and paved.

■ **Tuscobia Trail** – Built on old railroad tracks, the Tuscobia Trail shares a stretch with the Ice Age National Scenic Trail as it heads northeast. The trail runs about three miles to 22nd Street.

■ **Also see:** *Birchwood, Cameron/Chetek, Cumberland, Shell Lake/Sarona*

St. Croix Falls
Gandy Dancer State Trail segment

The Gandy Dancer State Trail runs roughly north-south for 98 miles with a number of accessible points in Wisconsin cabin country, making it ideal for a day hike. Built atop an old Minneapolis, St. Paul and Sault Ste. Marie railroad grade, the trail is named for the Gandy Tool Company workers who built the route back in the 1880s.

Paralleling State Hwy. 35, one of the easiest places to access the trail is in St. Croix Falls (the self-proclaimed and richly deserved "City of Trails") at the Polk County Information Center, located at the junction of U.S. Hwy. 8 and State

Hwy. 35. Parking is available at the info center.

The trail begins as paved asphalt then turns to packed crushed limestone, which makes for easy walking. As trains once needed to make their way where you'll walk, grade changes always are gradual.

A variety of trees often form a high canopy over the trail, offering plenty of shade and a real escape back to nature experience. This is especially so in autumn, when leaves change to form red, orange and golden roofs over hikers. In grassy areas, lupines, phlox and columbine flower during June.

When passing waterways, dragonflies frequently can be spotted during summer. Songbirds light most of the route with their melodies while squirrels scamper along the ground and up trees. Watch for white-tailed deer springing back into the woods when rounding curves.

The first segment of the trail runs 4.5 miles from the information center to the village of Centuria. If you have young children, you certainly don't have to walk the entire trail; mile posts signs along the way tell how far you've walked so you know when to turn around.

If your cabin is a little farther north, no worries. Running through nine villages and connecting with city parks, you can find a trailhead at several locations, including: Centuria, Milltown, Luck, Frederic, Lewis, Siren, Webster and Danbury. Those trail sections pass farmland, lakes and forests.

Bicyclists also are allowed to use the trail; be sure to keep an eye on children so they don't get in the way.

Indianhead Flowage Trail
St. Croix National Scenic Riverway

Your family can walk atop billion-year-old volcanic rock surrounded by the deep blue of a river and the lush green of a forest on the Indianhead Flowage Trail in the St. Croix National Scenic Riverway.

Located along State Hwy. 87 about a mile north of St. Croix Falls, the 1.5-long trail begins at Lion's Club Park. The trailhead is on the park road's southwest side.

That the path marks some of the opening miles of the Ice Age National Scenic Trail is appropriate. When the last glacier covering this region melted thousands of years ago, massive floods smashed through the area, carving the St. Croix River Valley out of volcanic basalt bedrock that formed some 750 million years before dinosaurs even existed.

The trail winds through forests and wetlands with bridges crossing streams flowing into the St. Croix River. At some spots, the trail comes within 20 feet of that waterway.

A warm, dry spring day marks an excellent time to hike the trail. Colorful wildflowers from trilliums and marsh marigolds to blue flag iris and wild geraniums carpet the area. In summer, the forest greenery dominates, but watch for trail-side raspberries in July.

A variety of migrating songbirds also can be heard during spring. Squirrels, chipmunks, whitetailed deer and raccoon abound as well through summer and autumn.

Be sure to carry insect repellent, however, as mosquitoes, deerflies and horseflies sometimes can be an annoyance. Always check for deer ticks after returning from the trail. Also, make sure kids stay on the trail, as poison ivy grows in the area (Remember: "Leaves of three, let it be.").

The handicap-accessible trail ends at a riverside campground. A primitive trail continues on but is not recommended for a day hike. Bathrooms, a playground, picnic area, and boat launch are located at Lion's Club Park.

Summit Rock Trail
Wisconsin Interstate State Park

On the scenic Summit Rock Trail, cabin-goers can hike across or see the results of the three most significant geological events to affect Wisconsin.

The trail takes hikers to the highest point at Interstate State Park in St. Croix Falls. It runs atop billion-year-old lava flows, the sands of a 500-million-year-old sea, and at the edge of a massive glacial flood from 10,000 years ago.

Interstate State Park sits off State Hwy. 35 just a half-mile mile south of U.S. Hwy. 8 along the St.

Croix River. There's an entrance fee, though a national park pass will get in you for free.

Follow Park Road into Interstate. As it heads south and reaches Lake of the Dalles, look for the parking lot on the road's right side. The trailhead is at the lot's north end.

Expect the park to be busy. It annually receives visitors on par with national parks. Additional parking lots can be found on the road's left side.

The trail heads to the bluff's highest point and is a dirt surface, so expect an uneven and steep walk at times. Small sections of the 0.5-mile long trail (one way) consist of stone and wooden steps through the wooden area.

Moss and autumn leaves cover the surrounding rock and ground. Maples, basswood and eastern white pines line the trail. At the top, prickly pear cactus even can be spotted amid the outcroppings.

Though the park includes a campground and is near an urban area, wildlife abounds. Expect to see squirrel, raccoon, deer and dozens of bird varieties along the way. Fox, muskrat and beaver live closer to the river.

The bluff wouldn't exist if not for a major geological event dating some 1.1 billion years ago. At that time, massive lava flows covered this region of the world. As you near the trail's top, the black basalt rock you pass and step upon dates from that era.

The highlight of the hike without question is the

incredible view of the riverway from the summit. Looking north, the Old Man of the Dalles rock formation is visible just beyond glacial potholes.

The rocks making up the Dalles actually were laid some 515 million years ago when this region sat under a warm shallow sea near the equator. As sediments piled up and were covered over the eons, they hardened into rock; the landscape finally rose above the sea about 345 million years ago.

Then about 10,000 years ago at the end of the last ice age (the third major geological event affecting Wisconsin), a glacial torrent swept through the area when ancient Lake Duluth drained south. This flood broke off the basalt in chunks, created the intriguing cliff formations, and gouged out the deep gorge that is now the river valley.

During the flood, giant eddies from the flow drilled holes into the landscape; these are the potholes between the summit and the Dalles. The largest glacial potholes in the world are just across the river in Minnesota.

Return to the parking lot the same way you came for a one-mile round trip. If you have a full day to spend, a plethora of other activities are held at the park; check at the visitor center for a schedule.

Nearby Trails

■ **Esker Trail** – This short trail runs atop a tall ridge of sediment left by the meltwater of a retreating glacier that was last seen in these parts some 10,000 years ago. The ridge offers fantastic views of the St. Croix River with visibility of up to eight miles on clear days.

■ **Ladder Tank Trail** – At the scenic riverway visitor's center, you can take 60 stairs to the top of a ridge for an overlook of the St. Croix. It's a short trail but pretty with a great view at the top.

■ **Pothole Trail** – When flood waters from melting glaciers swept through at the end of the last ice age, swirling water literally drilled holes into the basalt rock underlying this region. The 0.4-mile loop takes you past a number of these interesting geological features in Wisconsin Interstate Park. The park offers a variety of kid-friendly programs.

■**Riegel Park Trail** – The west end of Wisconsin's Ice Age National Scenic Trail starts with this trail at the village's 76-acre Riegel Park Preserve. A trap rock meadow covered in moss and lichen with scattered trees covers the preserve.

■ **River Bluff Trail** – This 0.7-mile trail in Wisconsin Interstate State Park takes hikers between the St. Croix River gorge and the Lake of the Dalles. The rocks and sparse vegetation gives it a Rocky Mountain feel.

■ **Rock Creek Trail** – Located about five miles east of town, the trail parallels its namesake through a 20-acre restored prairie. Boulders on the forested part of the trail were brought here by glaciers.

■ **Shadow and Angle rocks lookouts trails** – Across the border in Minnesota Interstate Park are a couple of sets of short trails that upon reaching the top offer great vistas of the St. Croix River and the gorge rock formation.

■ **Also see:** *Amery, Balsam Lake, Frederic/Luck, Osceola, Turtle Lake*

Shell Lake/Sarona

Bear Trail
Hunt Hill Audubon Sanctuary

Carnivorous plants and glacial lakes await hikers at the Hunt Hill Audubon Sanctuary in Washburn County.

Perhaps the best way to see the sanctuary's wide variety of ecosystems is the Bear Trail, a 2.7-mile loop to which this recommended hike adds a half-mile. Though owned by the National Audubon Society, the nonprofit Friends of Hunt Hill Audubon Sanctuary operates the facility, where it offers several quality educational programs.

Trails are open from dusk to dawn. Unlike state parks, entry is free for hiking. If able, though, help fill the donation boxes on the information kiosks. Late June marks a good time to visit because of the blooming orchids, but days can get humid and insect repellent suggested.

To reach the sanctuary, on U.S. Hwy. 53 between Sarona/Shell Lake and Spooner take County Road

B east. Turn right/south on County Road M then turn left/northwest onto Audubon Road. In about a mile, turn right/north on Hunt Hill Road. Go right/east at the first intersection and park at the cluster of buildings.

Continue walking east on the road that you parked your vehicle. At the end is the Vole Tail loop; go left on loop. To the south is a prairie where wildflowers abound in summer. You'll find the fairly even trail remains flat the rest of the way.

Sphagnum bog

Next you'll pass a sphagnum bog that borders Upper and Lower Twin Lakes. Unlike swamps, sphagnum bogs don't stink because of the water's high acidity.

In about a quarter of a mile, you'll come to the Bog Boardwalk, a 0.1-mile loop that takes you into the wetlands where you can see two carnivorous plants – the pitcher and the sundew. Such plants usually can be found in bogs and rock outcroppings, where the soil is nutrient poor, and make up for the loss by eating insects.

A number of plants live in the sphagnum bog; most notably, in late June showy orchids bloom. Other plants you'll find here include the arethusa, grass pink, pink lady's slipper, rose pogonia, sphagnum moss, and tamarack.

Continuing on Vole Trail, you'll parallel Lower Twin Lake. From here on out, the trail is heavily forested with mixed hardwoods and pines, providing pleasant shade on hot days.

The Twin Lakes formed some 10,000 years ago when a retreating glacier's chunk broke off. As sediment deposited around the melting ice, the lakes filled with water. Upper Twin Lake reaches an impressive depth of 53 feet.

Upon reaching Heron Point, the trail turns south. At the T-intersection, go left/northeast onto Bear Trail. You'll cross an old WCC footbridge over a beaver pond.

Watch for 240 birds

The trail then curves past Lower Twin Lake's southern-most edge and another bog. As you turn northeast, a small quarter mile loop – the Log Road Trail – juts off and then rejoins Bear Trail. This loop can be skipped.

As nearing Reed Lake, the trail curves northwest. Keep an eye out for osprey; a platform for the hunting bird sits on opposite shore.

If a bird watcher, Hunt Hill is the place to be. Up to 240 species of birds have been spotted here, including bald eagles, bluebirds, bobolinks, chickadees, the common loon, the Eastern meadowlark, the great egret, the green-backed heron, pheasant, the pileated woodpecker, the red owl, the red-shouldered hawk, the rose-breasted grosbeak, ruffed grouse, the sandhill crane, tree swallows, the veery, warblers, wild turkey, wood ducks, and wrens.

Leaving Reed Lake, you'll pass a bog between it and Big Devil's Lake. The trail then curves back toward Upper Twin Lake. The rise of land in the middle of the wetlands next to Lower Twin Lake is Osprey Isle, where there's another osprey platform.

The trail then jags in the opposite direction toward Big Devil's Lake. The 0.1-mile Big Devil's Lake Trail loops off the main route for a close-up of the waterbody and also can be skipped.

Common Northwoods mammals are likely to be seen on the Bear Trail. White-tailed deer, raccoons, squirrels and chipmunks abound. There's a bear's den nearby. Watch the trees for bite marks and girdling, a sign of porcupines.

Following the Big Devil's Lake shoreline for a while, the trail soon reaches Nordskog Footbridge at Wet Crossing. Take the new footbridge over a channel that connects Big Devil's Lake to Upper Twin Lake; before the bridge, hikers had to wade through the knee-deep stream.

The trail then skirts another bog next to Upper Twin Lake until coming to the Francis Andrews Trail. Go left onto the Francis Andrews back to the main cluster of buildings and your vehicle.

Nearby Trails

■ **Ice Age National Scenic Trail, Grassy Lake Segment** – This 7.2-mile section of the state-wide trail near Shell Lake can be accessed from Lehman Road. Part of the walk includes a ridge over a valley carved out by glacial meltwater.

■ **Sawyer Brook Springs trails** – A set of three loops, primarily maintained as cross-country ski trails, begin behind the Indian Arts Center in Shell Lake. The Yellow Loop takes hikers twice across Sawyer Brook Springs.

■ **South Side Walking Trail** – This comfortable path of wood chips works its way through meadows and wooded areas. The trail begins off of U.S. Hwy. 63 on Shell Lake's south side.

■ **Wild Rivers Trail segment** – This three-county trail runs along a former train route through Sarona on its way north from Barron County. Take the trail north to Spooner's Railroad Memories Museum.

■ **Also see:** *Birchwood, Cumberland, Frederic/ Luck, Rice Lake, Siren, Spooner*

Siren

Gandy Dancer State Trail segment

For a pleasant return to small town America, day hike the Gandy Dancer State Trail, which runs north-south through the village of Siren. Start downtown and head north to the airport for a four-mile round trip hike.

To reach the trail, park downtown in the northwest quadrant of the State Hwys. 35 and 70 intersection. The trail parallels Hwy. 35 so can be accessed by simply taking any street west. The village portion of the trail takes you back to Mayberry, to those long lost days when more of America lived in small rural towns than large cities. The trail here is fairly open, so be sure to wear a hat and sunscreen.

While in Siren, the trail crosses West Main Street, so exercise caution at this intersection, especially if children are with you.

Though Siren's population just tops 800, it's the Burnett County seat. The village's name is a misspelling of the Swedish word "siren," which means "lilac." The fragrant bush was common in the village when Swedish settlers established the town in the 1890s and still can be found aplenty more than 110 years later. Depending on how early spring arrives, the lilac blossoming makes May to June an excellent time to hike the trail.

After about two-thirds of a mile, you'll reach the edge of town. Though trees line the trail the entire way, they begin to grow thicker here.

To the right across the highway, you'll catch glimpses of Crooked Lake. You'll also hike past some lower-lying marshy stretches; as an old railroad bed, the trail is raised and wide, so there's no need to worry about wet feet.

After about 1.2 miles, forest entirely surrounds the trail. The trees are an excellent mix of red and sugar maples, oak, birch, basswood and pine.

You'll reach Airport Road after two miles; if

lucky, you may catch a small prop plane taking off or landing at the Burnett County Airport. While the trail continues north to Webster, the road marks a good spot to turn around.

Nearby Trails

■ **Amsterdam Sloughs Wildlife Area trails** – Located northwest of town, a jeep trail heads north into the wildlife area from Olsen Road, just west of Daniel Johnson Road. Turn back after reaching the pond for a 3.75-mile round trip.

■ **Ice Age National Scenic Trail** – Southeast of town at the end of 60th Street, follow a segment of this trail over the Clam River past Dinger Lake to McKenzie Creek. The 2.25-mile round trip cuts through mixed hardwood forests and meadows.

■ **Timberland Hills trails** – Southeast of town, Timberland Hills is in the Burnett County Forest off of County Road H. Mainly used as a ski trail in winter, during summer the connecting loops offer several miles of hiking trails.

■ **Also see:** *Grantsburg, Danbury, Frederic/Luck, Shell Lake/Sarona, Spooner, Webster*

Solon Springs

Brule Bog Boardwalk Trail
Brule River State Forest

Visitors to the Solon Springs area can day hike what feels like the forest primeval on the Brule Bog

Boardwalk Trail.

Located in southern Douglas County's Brule River State Forest, the 2.3-mile boardwalk cuts through a wooded bog. Part of the North Country National Scenic Trail, it is entirely handicapped accessible.

To reach the trail, from downtown Solon Springs take County Highway A north for about three miles, rounding the northern side of Upper St. Croix Lake. Watch for signs saying the North Country Trail is "1000 Feet Ahead," then turn into the boat landing where you can park.

Across the road from the parking lot, the trail heading right/northeast is the Brule-St. Croix Portage Trail (see below). The boardwalk trail heads left or directly north.

An elevated boardwalk takes hikers through a conifer swamp at the bottom of a narrow valley. The valley marks a continental divide – all rivers to the south ultimately feed the Mississippi River while those to the north flow into Lake Superior, which is part of the St. Lawrence watershed.

In short order, the boardwalk crosses St. Croix Creek. You've now entered the heart of Brule Bog. Ferns and mosses, as well as several varieties of orchids, cover the ground while white cedar, balsam fir, and spruce crowd out the sunlight.

Several rare plants and animals can be found in the bog. Among the insects you'll quickly notice is the zebra clubtail dragonfly. Songbirds include the

black-backed woodpecker, golden-crowned king-
let, Lincoln's sparrow, olive-sided flycatcher, and
saw-whet owl. Plants include the sheathed and the
sparse-flowered sedge and the endangered Lap-
land buttercup.

The sense of having traveled back in time to the
ancient Carboniferous Period is temporarily inter-
rupted as the trail crosses County Road P, which
runs smack down the bog's middle.

After the county road, the boardwalk trail veers
northwest. You'll come to the edge of the bog
against a hillside, where the trail begins to mean-
der. The uplands above the bog consist of sandy
pine barrens.

Some 9,000 years ago as the last ice age ended,
a river flowing out of the much higher glacial Lake
Superior carved out the valley where the Brule River, this bog, and Upper St. Croix Lake now exist.
Released from the retreating glacier's weight, the
land rose, causing water to flow in different directions and hence the divide.

The boardwalk ends at a spur off of Croshaw
Road. This is the turnaround point.

A final note: You'll definitely want to apply insect
repellant before hitting this trail.

Nearby Trails

■ **Brule-St. Croix Portage Trail** – People have
used this trail for hundreds of years, most notably
beginning in 1680 when French explorer Daniel

Greysolon Sieur duLhut first noted the route linking the Brule and St. Croix rivers. It's an easy 4.4-mile out-and-back trail with minimal elevation gain.

■ **North Country National Scenic Trail-Douglas County Forest segment** – South of town, the seven-state North Country Trail crosses the Douglas County Forest for roughly three miles. It passes several idyllic ponds along the way.

■ **North Country National Scenic Trail-segment through town** – Before reaching the county forest, the trail cuts through the village. A pleasant two-mile route runs south of town to the county forest from South Holly Lucius Road/U.S. Hwy. 53 to Bird Sanctuary Road at the forest's edge.

■ **Wild Rivers State Trail segment** – The rail line turned hiking path also runs through the village on its way between Gordon and Superior. To avoid highway noise, take the roughly four-mile route heading north from the municipal airport to County Road L.

■ **Also see:** *Drummond, Minong, Poplar/Brule, Superior*

Somerset

Parnell Prairie Preserve loops
Parnell Prairie Preserve

Hikers at the Parnell Prairie Preserve west of Somerset can see an ecosystem in the making as a long-abandoned dump is reclaimed. In fact, you might consider repeated trips here during the years ahead to watch the prairie spring alive.

The preserve is fairly new, opening in 2010 as a park jointly operated by the Township and Village of Somerset. In all, you'll walk less than a half-mile on its trails, though there are some side loops that allow you to add a few extra steps if you're up to it.

As you're walking across an open meadow, there's little sun cover; because of this, morning and early evening are best for hiking. Regardless the time of day, though, you'll definitely want to bring a hat. The preserve is open 5 a.m.-10 p.m. daily.

To reach the preserve, from Somerset head west/south on State Hwy. 64. At the village's edge, turn left/west onto 180th Avenue. In about 2.5 miles at 38th Street, 180th Avenue goes right/north. At the tee intersection, go right/east onto 44th Street, which curves and becomes 45th Street.

As the road straightens, turn right into the parking lot.

None of the trails are named and are mainly loops sharing common segments. You'll find getting lost difficult, though; the preserve is an open area and largely bordered by trees.

The trailhead of this recommended hike is at the northeast corner of the parking lot and goes straight east into the prairie. Mowed trails cross rolling terrain.

For 21 years – from 1967-88, this site served as

the Somerset "town dump." The area previously had been farmed by Albert (Alley) Parnell, whose forefathers were among this region's original pioneer families. After the dump closed, officials covered the 5.5-acre refuse site with two feet of fine-grained soils and then six inches of topsoil. The land sat vacant for several years, then in 2010, the U.S. Fish and Wildlife Service began restoring the prairie.

In about 250 feet, the trail comes to a junction. Go left/northeast with the trail curving to the preserve's north side. As walking, you may notice the dirt beneath the grass is particularly poor for Wisconsin. This medium textured and moderately coarse soil is typical of outwash plains created as the glaciers retreated from this area some 10,000 years ago.

After about 200 feet, you'll come to another junction. This time, go right/southeast for 150 feet. The soil and flat terrain make good growing conditions for cool season prairie grasses. The current restoration plan calls for making the entire area look like some of the small prairie remnants along the railroad tracks bordering the preserve's south side.

At the next junction, go right/south. This takes you to roughly the center of the preserve. After 100 feet, the trail swerves northeast.

The area specifically is a dry mesic prairie, in which tall species such as big bluestem and Indian-grass typically dominate. Herbs also are common-place. Such prairies used to run all through south-ern Wisconsin, but most were plowed under dec-ades ago for farmland. Less than 1 percent of the state's dry mesic prairies remain.

In 400 more feet, you'll arrive at another junc-tion. You're now at the preserve's eastern edge. Turn right/southwest to begin the loop back home.

Though the restoration has only begun, you'll probably spot some of the animals that typically live in a dry mesic area. Butterflies are abundant in summertime. Among the many birds are barn owls, bobolinks, dickcissel, Eastern and Western meadowlarks, grasshopper sparrow, greater prair-ie-chicken, Henslow's sparrow, and the upland sandpiper. Common mammals include Franklin's ground squirrel, prairie vole, and the white-tailed jackrabbit.

For the next 750 feet or so, the trail meanders but roughly parallels the preserve's eastern and southern woodline of pines. At the junction, go left/west (i.e. straight). The trail curves toward the woodline; if a sunny day, you're likely to get some good cover here, and your location gives you a good, broad view of the sweeping meadow.

When the restoration is completed, the prairie likely will appear just as it did in the mid-1800s to Parnell's ancestors and other pioneers of this area. Indeed, a government survey report from August 1847 reports that the area's southern edge was void of trees and had second-rate soil.

After another 300 feet, the trail curves north. It's another 150 feet or so to the parking lot.

Nearby Trails

■ **La Grandeur Natural Area Trail** – This short trail in the La Grandeur Natural Area, located at the village's northeast side, wraps around the water tower and pond to the west. A jeep trail largely skirts the wooded area.

■ **Mound (White) Trail** – South of Somerset is an often overlooked section of Willow River State Park. The 1.1-mile Mound Trail offers views of the Willow River and a glacial mound (a hill that resisted erosion during the last ice age) on the opposite shore.

■ **New Richmond Heritage Center/Paperjack Creek Trail** – East of Somerset in the city of New Richmond, hikers can combine a walk near a stream with a loop through a historical village and farm that show what life was like in western Wisconsin during decades ago.

■ **Also see:** *Amery, Clear Lake, Hudson, Osceola*

Spooner

Beaver Brook East Trail
Beaver Brook Wildlife Area

Cabin-goers in the Spooner-Shell Lake area can enjoy a pleasant hike along a classic trout stream on Beaver Brook Wildlife Area's East Trail. Along the way, you may spot the impressive osprey or bald eagle.

The wildlife area nicely preserves 1,964 acres of woods and wetlands between Shell Lake and Spooner. A number of loops run off the main trail so hikers can adjust the walk's length to meet their time restrictions and energy levels. Dogs also are allowed on the trail.

The wildlife area boasts multiple access points. To reach the East Trail, from Spooner head south on U.S. Hwy. 53. Turn south onto Cranberry Drive. After about a mile, just before road curves southeast away from Beaver Brook, turn into the parking lot. This places you at about the wildlife area's center.

Spring-pond fed stream

From the parking lot's northeast corner, head north paralleling Cranberry Drive then veer away from the road for a half mile to trail junction B. A 0.8-mile trail loops off here; it rejoins the main trail at junction C.

Most of the trail runs beneath mixed hardwoods, such as maple, oak and aspen. There's some conifer, pine and tamarack as well as red oak stands.

Continuing ahead on the main trail, you'll begin following Beaver Brook for a half mile to trail junction D. There, you can get a close look at the stream in a 0.4-mile loop that rejoins the main trail at junction E. Beaver Brook stands out as a Class I brook and brown trout stream. Well-shaded (the brook doesn't show up on satellite maps), 10 spring ponds and a number of bank seeps feed it as it heads north into the Yellow River Flowage.

If you skip this loop, the distance between trail junctions D and E is 0.2 miles. At trail junction E, you'll pass the brook's largest spring pond on the trail's left side.

Dive fishing

Keep an eye out for a number of birds, who either appreciate the wooded cover or the brook's fish. Among the former are the American woodcock, ruffed grouse, and various waterfowl. Among the latter are bald eagles and the North American osprey.

Osprey can reach up to two feet in length with a wingspan of more than five feet. They feed on pan and sucker fish, and if lucky, you may see it dive for one. Osprey typically fly their search patterns some 30-100 feet above the stream and upon spotting prey dive feet first into the water. Once a fish is caught, their feet juggle it around until the prey's head faces the wind. They then take it to their perch and feed.

Beyond birds, white-tailed deer, squirrels and chipmunks are ubiquitous here.

After 0.75 miles, you'll come to trail junction G and another loop with a variety of options. Going right means you'll walk roughly northeast back toward Hwy. 53 for 0.68 miles. You'll hear a small amount of freeway noise, but it's momentary, as you curve away from it.

At trail junction I, you can either:

■ Go left for 0.43 miles to trail junction H; from there, go left for 0.06 miles back to trail junction G and return the way you came.

■ Continue straight, looping about 1.12 miles to trail junction G (you'll pass trail junction H along the way), and then return the parking lot the way you came.

In the winter, these are ski trails with specific rules about which direction you should go on each loop. These directions aren't particularly relevant for day hikers, though.

Before heading onto the trail, you may want to stop at a local bookstore and pick up Spooner author Peter Hubin's "A Brook Runs through It." His novel is set along Beaver Brook.

Nearby Trails

■ **College Street City Park Trail** – Several loops run through Spooner City Park at the end of College Street. One route encircles the park.

■ **Nordic Woods A Loop** – From County Board B at the north tip of Long Lake, follow the entry trail to the A Loop for a 2.7-mile excursion. Shadow Lake is a short walk away on another loop.

■ **Ridge Walking Trails** – Nineteen miles east of

town in Stone Lake, these trails ramble through the 17.4-acre Stone Lake Wetland Park. The park also offers a 600-foot boardwalk and covered walking bridge.

■ **Wild Rivers Trail** – This three-county trail runs through Spooner on its way from Sarona to Trego. Heading south is the prettier route; start at the city's Railroad Memories Museum on Front Street for a 3.8-mile one way walk to the Beaver Brook Wildlife Area.

■ **Also see:** *Danbury, Hayward, Shell Lake/Sarona, Siren, Trego, Webster*

Superior

Big Manitou Falls overlook trails
Pattison State Park

Just a few miles south of the largest metro area of northern Minnesota and Wisconsin flows the highest waterfall in either state. Short overlook trails in Pattison State Park offer a variety of scenic views of Big Manitou Falls.

Summer marks the most comfortable time to visit the falls, but each season offers a unique experience. Winter means offers rising off the falls, spring brings thundering water flows, and autumn reveals the fantastic ancient rocks forming the gorge below.

To reach the park, take State Hwy. 35 south about 13 miles from Superior. The entrance and parking lot is on the left. A $5 entry fee is required per vehicle.

For the trailhead, head to the southwest corner of the parking lot and take the pathway through the park's grassy picnic area past the nature center toward Interfalls Lake. Even though trees block the waterfalls, you'll be able to hear its rumble.

At the lake, follow the pedestrian tunnel under Hwy. 35. The half-mile-long trail's difficulty level is easy with minimal elevation gain.

Past the tunnel, stay on the north side of Black River, which the Ojibwa Indians who once lived here called "Mucudewa Sebee," translating to "dark." It aptly describes the brown-tinted river, the coloration caused by decaying leaves and roots spilling into the waterway.

Short trails leading off the main one give you two views of Big Manitou Falls. At 165 feet, the falls is the fourth largest east of the Rockies and the same height as Niagara.

The falls exists because of the dark basalt, the remains of a 1.2-billion-year-old lava flow that covers much of the Wisconsin-Minnesota border area. The Douglas Fault runs downstream from the falls, with the southern side of the fault rises at a 50 degree angle. Today, Black River runs down this gorge formed long ago by volcanic action and earthquakes, eventually meeting the Nemadji River, which flows into Lake Superior.

A century ago, developers almost wiped out the

falls with a planned hydroelectric dam. The park's namesake, Martin Pattison, purchased land to deliberately block the dam's construction, however.

For a longer walk and additional views of the falls, head back toward the tunnel but before reaching it take a connecting trail that heads across the river. This provides two additional views from the south.

Though you'll probably be focused on the falls, keep an eye out for the local wildlife in this boreal forest. More than 200 bird species, including hawks and owls, as well 50-plus mammals, such as porcupines and black bears, call the park home.

On the way back to your vehicle, stop at the Gitchee Gummee Nature Center for its exhibits. The popular state park also hosts nature programs and boasts a sandy beach. For children, the nature center loans out two different nature exploration backpacks full of fun activities. Pets on a leash are allowed.

Also, this is a carry in/carry out park, so you'll have trouble finding garbage cans.

Nearby Trails

■ **Gandy Dancer State Trail segment** – This interstate trail re-enters Wisconsin from Minnesota south of Superior and runs for 15 minutes until joining the Saunders State Trail. A pleasant 2.85-mile stretch runs from South Foxboro-Chaffey Road over Balsam Creek to Drolson Road.

■ **Millennium Trail** – The 1.6-mile trail runs from Billings Drive to Elmira Avenue in the Superior Municipal Forest on the city's southwest side. The trailhead is at the 28th Street and Wyoming Avenue intersection.

■ **Osaugie Trail** – Beautiful views of Superior Bay, a marina, and city piers abound on this urban trail, which runs for five miles from Marina Drive at the U.S. Hwys. 2/53 junction south to Moccasin Mike Road. It is wheelchair accessible.

■ **Pokegama Trail** – Also in the municipal forest, this 6.14-mile trail is popular with cyclists (a local cycling club actually maintains the trail). The trailhead is north of Central Avenue east of the Cemetery Access Road intersection.

■ **Saunders State Trail segment** – The 8-mile trail runs southwest of town through several small communities. Try the 3.3-mile segment from County Road W north of Dewey to the bridge at Clear Creek; the route crosses the Pokegama River.

■ **Tri-County Corridor Trail segment** – The well-maintained trail with a crushed limestone surface links Superior to Ashland. Pick up the trail at 57th Avenue where the Osaugie Trail meets it and turn around at the second stream crossing for a 2.3-mile round trip.

■ **Wild Rivers State Trail, Amnicon River segment** – The 104-mile trail from Rice Lake finds its terminus here (or depending on your perspective, it's beginning). Head southeast of the city to

Swamp Road for a 5.4-mile out-and-back hike across the Amnicon River and two other waterways to Mikrot Road.

■ **Also see:** *Danbury, Iron River, Poplar/Brule, Solon Springs*

Trego
Trego River Trail
St. Croix National Scenic Riverway

A pleasant walk through the woods along a wild river await hikers on the Trego Nature Trail in the St. Croix National Scenic Riverway.

Located in Washburn County, the trail is best done during summer when the shaded walk keeps hikers cool. Early fall is a good time for those who enjoy fall colors.

To reach the trail, take U.S. Hwy. 63 north of Trego village. About 1.3 miles from the visitor center and after crossing the bridge over the Namekagon River, take the first right. The parking lot is at the end of this entrance road.

Look for the trailhead on the parking lot's east side. The trail is fairly well-maintained. Watch for some steep inclines and narrow sections on curves, however.

The trail parallels the Namekagon River through a woods of pines and deciduous trees, with views of the waterway. Benches typically sit in the view-spots.

Hikers are likely to see a variety of wildlife or at least signs of it. White-tailed deer, turtles, fox, muskrat, bobcats, squirrels, snowshoe hares, and the great blue heron abound in the riverway. Watch for otters and their slides, muddy paths cleared in the river's bank in which they move from land to water.

You also might spot lake sturgeon, Wisconsin's largest fish, especially if the water is low. They like to lay motionless beneath overhanging trees. In fact, the river's name comes from the Ojibwe Indian words that loosely mean "place of the sturgeon." Most of the sturgeon, however, are downriver below the Trego Dam.

After the footbridge, the trail loops back upon itself. Hikers can return to the parking lot the same way they came in. The trail comes to about 2.8 miles round trip.

Dogs are allowed on the trail if leashed. For safety, don't climb the river banks, as they can be slick.

On the drive back home, stop at the Namekagon Visitor Center for displays about the riverway.

Nearby Trails

■ **Leisure Lake Trail** – Northwest of town, a 3-mile trail heads about Leisure Lake, off of Skunk Lake Road. The lake's shoreline is nicely forested.

■ **Trego Lake Trail** – A trio of loops run for 3.5 miles near the Namekagon River and Trego Lake in the St. Croix National Scenic Riverway. A combination of the A and B loops offer the best river and lake views.

■ **Wild Rivers Trail** – The former C&NW Rail route turned hiking trail runs through town from Spooner to Minong. From Park Street, take an almost 2-mile round trip walk north through the St. Croix National Scenic Riverway, including a bridge over the Namekagon River.

■ **Also see:** *Danbury, Hayward, Minong, Spooner*

Turtle Lake
Cattail State Trail (Turtle Lake to Almena segment)

Active railroad lines once crisscrossed northwestern Wisconsin's beautiful countryside, but the advent of highways made many of them obsolete. A number of those old tracks fortunately have been converted to hiking trails so that modern day walkers can enjoy a plethora of scenery from woodlands to rolling pastures.

Among them is the Cattail State Trail, which runs for nearly 18 miles on an old Soo Line rail bed between Amery and Almena with access in Turtle Lake. Its location is perfect for a number of cabingoers in Polk and Barron counties.

To reach the trail, Take U.S. Hwy. 8 to any of the above mentioned communities. The trailhead is on Keller Avenue South (State Hwy. 46) near Baker

Street West in Amery, behind the village hall (where you can park) in Turtle Lake, and on Alma Street in Almena.

Turtle Lake serves as a great starting point, since you can break the trail into smaller sections by going either toward Amery or Almena. The Turtle Lake access also is a block from Railway Park, which includes a picnic shelter. Head west toward Amery for wetlands and a thick woods, both of which teem with wildlife, including white-tailed deer, otter, mink, fox, eagles, osprey a couple of hundred bird species and even black bear. This five-mile section of the trail running to the village of Joel also is open to horses.

If starting in Amery, the trail begins in woodland then passes through farmland and prairie. Beaver Creek runs alongside the trail as closing on Joel.

In Almena, a 16-mile extension heads east to Cameron. Though pretty, this direction generally is not great for hikers, though, as three miles into the extension is an expansive area popular with ATVers. The extension also closes around mid-October for hunting.

Crushed stone covers the main trail, and the old rail line is smooth with the most gradual of elevation gains. The trail boasts six bridges. It does cross several roads, however, so be careful at these intersections, especially if with children. The trail also is open to dogs, which is great for many families. Dogs must be on a leash, though.

Nearby Trails

■ **Joel Marsh Wildlife Area jeep trail** – Berry picking and wildlife watching are popular activities on this wildlife area; among the first pair of nesting trumpeter swans were located here in 1991. An old jeep trail begins where the main road ends south of Joel Flowage and runs for almost a mile to 120th Avenue.

■ **Loon Lake State Wildlife Area trail** – Along the oddly named 18-1/2 19-1/2 Avenue is a trail heading east through woodlands to a pond. The wildlife area is an excellent place for birdwatching with around 140 species spotted.

■ **Silver Creek County Forest trails** – A number of trails run through this forest south of the village; a good one begins at the end of 5-1/2 Street and parallels Turtle Creek for a 1-mile round trip.

■ **Skinaway Lake Recreational Park trails** – On the north side of town, a trail makes its way through a mixed hardwood forest along the shores of Skinaway Lake. The lake is popular for its largemouth bass and several varieties of panfish.

■ **Also see:** *Amery, Balsam Lake, Cameron/Chetek, Clear Lake, Cumberland, St. Croix Falls*

Washburn

Teuton Trail Loop C
Chequamegon National Forest

Day hikers during summer can enjoy a set of

trails that the U.S. Olympic Nordic Ski Team once trained on near Washburn.

A pair of three loops – the Teuton and the Valkyrie – make up the Mt. Valhalla trails in the Chequamegon National Forest. A shortened version of the Teuton Trail System's Loop C makes for a somewhat challenging 2.75-mile hike.

To reach the trail, from Washburn take County Road C north for 8.5 miles. The parking lot is on the road's south side, where the Teuton Trail is located (The Valkyrie Trail is on the north side of the road.); you'll need a pass to park your vehicle in the national forest.

From the parking lot, follow the trail clockwise (the opposite way skiers take it), by heading south past the shelter. Upon reaching the split in trail, go left/southeast, putting you on Loop C.

From there, you'll begin traveling along the side of Mt. Valhalla and soon cross Four Mile Creek. The trail ultimately climbs about 170 feet in elevation with few level areas.

You may be too busy taking in Mt. Valhalla's natural beauty to notice. The trail runs through a Northern hardwood forest – rare for the Bayfield Peninsula – full of big tooth aspen, black oak, paper birch, and sugar maple trees, with a few scattered Eastern white pines. Ferns blanket the forest floor.

After a quarter mile, the trail begins to curve south then west. You'll soon parallel Four Mile

Creek and then cross it again. A variety of frogs, chipmunks and red squirrels inhabit this area, and you're likely to see if not hear them on the trail.

In another mile, the trail curves north. Keep an ear out for the many songbirds in the forest, including the yellow-bellied sapsucker, blue jays, wood thrush, robins, warblers, sparrows, and grosbeaks.

After about a quarter mile when you come to a trail junction, go right/east. You're now on Loop B. As the trail turns sharp to the north, you'll come the closest to reaching Mt. Valhalla's summit. The mountain tops out at 1388 feet, and you'll be about 110 feet below it.

Though technically not a mountain, Mt. Valhalla appears high given the Bayfield Peninsula's fairly flat terrain. But it's not even the highest point in the county; the tallest is Mt. Telemark at 1700 feet.

Loop B meanders downhill in a northerly direction for about 0.75 miles. The trail then takes a hard right for 0.5 miles with Loop A joining it along the way. This will take you back to the parking lot.

Don't worry about getting confused by all of the trail junctions and intersecting snowmobile trails that cross your route. All of the Teuton's loops are well-signed, and a metal map is at every junction.

Nearby Trails

■ **Big Rock County Park trails** – Trails ramble through the park, split in half by a first-class steelhead trout stream, the Sioux River. Wildlife sightings are a certainty for hikers.

■ **Birch Grove Campground Trail** – Located in the Chequamegon National Forest at the campground, the trail circles East Twin Lake for a 1-mile loop. Trailheads are located at both boat landings.

■ **Henkens Road Walking trails** – Two trails can be found off Henkins Road about 1.5 miles from the Star Route Road intersection northwest of town. A trailhead is located on each side of the road.

■ **Houghton Falls Trail** – You can walk across an ancient riverbed and see fascinating rock formations up close north of town at the Houghton Falls Nature Preserve.

■ **Washburn Lakefront Walking Trail** – In town, the 1.34-mile trail runs along Lake Superior, passing three beaches, the picturesque marina, and several historical sites. The trail connects Thompson West End Park and Memorial Park.

■ **Washburn School Forest and Environmental Education Center trails** – Ski trails can be used as hiking trails in summer in this heavily wooded center. The forest is on Eighth Avenue West.

■ **Also see:** *Ashland, Bayfield, Drummond, Iron River*

Webster

Gandy Dancer State Trail segment

A scenic segment of the Gandy Dancer State

Trail runs for two miles north of Webster from the Yellow River to Yellow Lake at Lone Pine Road.

As with most rail lines turned hiking trails, the former Minneapolis, St. Paul, and Sault Ste. Marie Railroad corridor is flat. And despite that this section in Burnett County is close to built-up areas, it's fairly tranquil.

To reach this segment of the trail, take State Hwy. 35 north of town. Just across the Yellow River at the Yellow River Saloon and Eatery, turn left; park in the gravel lot. Access the trail by heading west on the road just north of this establishment. A 900-foot walk leads to the trail at the Yellow River's edge.

Most of the trail is wooded, but there are some open, unshaded stretches, so be sure to wear a hat and sunscreen.

About a half mile from the Yellow River, the Gandy Dancer crosses a jeep trail then 400 feet later a gravel road. Watch for vehicles on the roads, especially if children are with you.

For the next 0.75 miles, the trail becomes forested and shaded. A good mix of maples, oaks, aspens and pine grow in the wooded area.

The trail then crosses Jeffries Road, so again exercise caution, as this is a busier street than the previous two.

While the trail remains wooded north of the road, the surrounding area is a bit more built up as you near Yellow Lake. About 0.4 miles from the road, you should be able to see the lake itself as the trail skirts its eastern shore.

At 2,283 acres, Yellow Lake sports a mean depth of 19 feet. It's a popular fishing lake for catfish, largemouth and smallmouth bass, musky, Northern pike, panfish, sturgeon and walleye.

Upon crossing at Finlayson Road, the trail swerves away from the lake. When you've reached Lone Pine Road, you've gone about two miles, marking a good spot to turn back.

Nearby Trails

■ **Amsterdam Sloughs Wildlife Area trails** – A jeep trail parallels County Road D in the forest's northwest corner. On the 4.8-mile round trip hike, part of which is alongside a lake, expect to spot blue heron, osprey and even signs of bear.

■ **Keizer Lake Wildlife Area East-West trail** – A jeep trail runs about 1.3 miles one way east-west through the wildlife area. It's easiest to find from the east terminus, as it's the only entry along County Road A. Watch the skies for bald eagles and osprey.

■ **Also see:** *Danbury, Grantsburg, Siren, Spooner, Trego*

Index

About the Author

Rob Bignell is a long-time hiker, journalist and author of the popular "Hikes with Tykes" guidebooks and several other titles. He and his son Kieran have been hiking together for the past five years. Before Kieran, Rob served as an infantryman in the Army National Guard and taught middle school students in New Mexico and Wisconsin. His newspaper work has won several national and state journalism awards, from editorial writing to sports reporting. In 2001, The Prescott Journal, which he served as managing editor of, was named Wisconsin's Weekly Newspaper of the Year. Rob and Kieran live in Hudson, Wis.

CHECK OUT THESE OTHER HIKING BOOKS BY ROB BIGNELL

"Hikes with Tykes" series:
◆Hikes with Tykes: A Practical Guide to Day Hiking with Children
◆Hikes with Tykes: Games and Activities

"Hittin' the Trail" ebooks:
◆Amnicon Falls State Park (Wis.)
◆Apostle Islands National Seashore
◆Ashland County, Wis.
◆Barron County, Wis.
◆Bayfield County, Wis.
◆Burnett County, Wis.
◆Chequamegon National Forest
◆Douglas County, Wis.
◆Interstate State Park (Minn./Wis.)
◆Pattison State Park (Wis.)
◆Polk County, Wis.
◆St. Croix County, Wis.
◆St. Croix Falls, Wis.
◆St. Croix National Scenic Riverway
◆Sawyer County, Wis.
◆Washburn County, Wis.
◆William O'Brien State Park (Minn.)
◆Willow River State Park (Wis.)

ORDER THEM ONLINE AT:
hikeswithtykes.com/hittinthetrail_home.html

WANT MORE INFO ABOUT FAMILY DAY HIKES?

Follow this book's blog, where you'll find:

Tips on day hiking with kids

Lists of great trails to hike with children

Parents' questions about
day hiking answered

Product reviews

Games and activities for the trail

News about the book series
and author

Visit online at:
hikeswithtykes.blogspot.com

Made in the USA
Monee, IL
16 March 2022

92968363R00095